INDEPENDENT VOTERS WILL DECIDE AMERICA'S FUTURE IN 2024 AND BEYOND

WHAT YOU SHOULD KNOW BEFORE VOTING

By Charles Steven Konigsberg

Independent Voter and Veteran Policy Adviser and Counsel to Senators, White House officials, and Agency Heads of Both Political Parties

A publication of Capitol Public Policy LLC

A Publication of Capitol Public Policy LLC

For information about this publication or speaking engagements by the author: independentvoters2024@gmail.com

ISBN: 9798337513393 (pbk)
ISBN: 9798337515632 (hcv)

PREFACE FOR
INDEPENDENT VOTERS

(Read Time: 2 minutes)

Nearly half of Americans today identify as independent voters—as reflected in the Gallup graph below. Independent voters will have a major impact on the outcome of the 2024 presidential election—the most consequential election in recent memory.

As an independent, you are a special voter. You will not enter the voting booth and reflexively vote for one party or the other. You look at the issues and the facts and make an independent judgment on which candidates are best able to develop solutions and work cooperatively to move the country forward.

Like you, I am an independent voter. I have supported presidential candidates of both political parties. In my public service career, I have served as a senior adviser for U.S. Senators, White House officials, and agency heads of **both political parties**. I believe in putting the country ahead of party and problem-solving with facts—not ideology.

The challenge we face in the internet age is sifting through the constant flood of information and misinformation, facts and distractions, to make a sound choice on election day.

I have prepared this short, nonpartisan book to provide independent voters with a **factual comparison** of the records of the last two Administrations—with Trump as President and Harris as Vice President—as you decide how to vote in this pivotal 2024 election. The book indicates where Harris' proposed policies depart from those of the current Administration (based on policies released through the end of the Democratic Convention).

The decisions made by a Harris or Trump Administration will directly impact *your family, your finances, your healthcare, your job, your freedom to make personal decisions, and the stability of our country—both domestically and internationally.*

It is my hope that this factual, nonpartisan account of the Trump and Harris records in office, and their most recent statements on key issues, will assist you in exercising your decisive role as an independent voter.

This book is laid out in 16 short sections, beginning with polling results you will find encouraging: **large majorities of Americans remain far more united on core values than media and politicians would have us believe.** The book then lays out the factual records of the Trump and Biden-Harris Administrations, and recent statements by Trump and Harris, on today's key issues: the economy, immigration, Social Security, Medicare, affordable healthcare and housing, education, abortion, crime, defense and global stability, veterans, coping with climate-induced floods and wildfires, infrastructure and energy independence, poverty, and preserving our democracy and Constitution.

Following this preface is a short summary of the 16 sections, so you can select which sections are of greatest interest to you (and the average reading time for each section); or you can read the entire book in one evening.

Each fact presented in this book is drawn from *reputable, nonpartisan sources* and is clearly referenced and hyperlinked in the end notes for e-Book readers and on the book's website for print readers (IndependentVotersBook.com).

Finally, please tell other independent voters about this book. If there is sufficient interest, there will be follow-up projects for independent voters, aimed at electing candidates to Congress and other public offices who are more focused on common sense and collaborative problem-solving than advancing their own ideological, extreme agendas.

Charles S. Konigsberg,
August 26, 2024

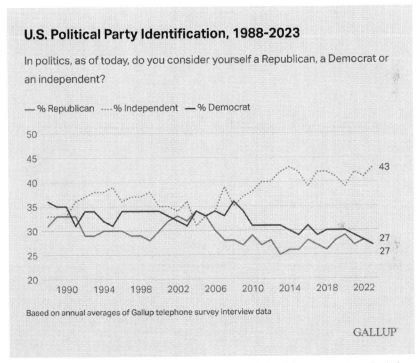

Reprinted with Permission from Gallup. Original image and underlying data are available at: https://news.gallup.com/poll/548459/independent-party-tied-high-democratic-new-low.aspx.

Contents

SUMMARY

(Read Time: 8 minutes)

Summary of sections:

1. **America is not hopelessly divided; polls in 2024 show large majorities of Americans continue to share core values**— equal protection under the laws; the right to vote; the freedoms of speech, press and assembly; freedom of religion without government interference; the right to privacy without government intrusion; and the opportunity to earn a place in America's middle class. *(Section 1—read time: 10 minutes.)*

2. **The Economy: Trump's policies risk more inflation, threaten economic stability.** Sixteen Nobel-laureate economists issued a warning in June 2024 that Donald Trump's policies would likely "reignite…inflation with his fiscally irresponsible budgets" and Trump's failure to adhere to the rule of law and international norms would threaten the U.S. economy's global position.[1] Moreover, as explained in §2 of this book, Trump's tax proposals would further explode an already risky public debt, as he did during his first term. *(Section 2—read time: 27 minutes.)*

3. **Immigration: Illegal southern border crossings are no longer at crisis levels.**[2] However, Donald Trump's promised expulsion of 11 million people would create an unnecessary economic crisis. Section 3 of this book clears up a flood of misinformation, distortions, and fearmongering about immigration,

while clearly explaining how the system actually works. *(Section 3—read time: 24 minutes.)*

4. **Middle Class Relief: Housing, Child Care, Student Loans, and Medical Debt.** As detailed in §4, Kamala Harris would extend tax relief for the middle class, restore and expand the child tax credit, extend and make permanent expanded Affordable Care Act subsidies for health insurance, provide new tax credits for first-time home buyers, take actions to slow the increase in home and rental prices, extend the solvency of Social Security and Medicare, reduce prescription drug prices, remove medical debt from credit reports, provide student loan debt relief, and reduce child care costs. Donald Trump's policies would trigger hyper-inflation—squeezing the middle class economically. He opposes student loan debt relief. He is likely to resume first-term efforts to repeal the Affordable Care Act, causing millions of low- and middle-income Americans to lose health insurance coverage. *(Section 4—read time: 12 minutes.)*

5. **Social Security:** The Social Security Trust Funds will be unable to pay full benefits by 2033 because benefits will exceed revenues. Donald Trump's policy proposals would push the Trust Funds into insolvency faster by depleting payroll tax revenues. The Biden-Harris Administration has proposed increasing payroll taxes on the wealthy to extend the life of the Trust Funds. *(Section 5—read time: 5 minutes.)*

6. **Healthcare: Protecting Medicare and Expanding Affordable Care:** Current estimates are that Medicare Hospital Insurance (HI) will be unable to pay full benefits by 2036 and the escalating *overall costs* of the Medicare program will drive up the public debt. Donald Trump's plans would deplete the Medicare HI Trust Fund faster by cutting payroll tax revenues, while the Biden-Harris Administration has proposed steps to extend the Trust Fund, and reduce overall Medicare spending by reducing prescription drug costs. With respect to affordable

care, Donald Trump's repeated, failed efforts in his first term to "repeal and replace" the Affordable Care Act ("ACA") would have cut off affordable healthcare for millions. He now promises to make the ACA "better" but has no proposals to do so. The Biden-Harris Administration has *increased* health care coverage in America to record levels. *(Section 6—read time: 18 minutes.)*

7. **Housing Affordability for Renters and Buyers:** Most Americans are concerned about the affordability of housing. As President, Trump proposed massive cuts to federal affordable housing programs for low-income Americans, which provide vital rent subsidies and other low-cost housing options. Harris has rolled out proposals to incentivize an increase in the supply of housing, assist first-time homebuyers, and slow the increase in home prices and rentals. *(Section 7—read time: 6 minutes.)*

8. **Education: Grade School & Vaccinations, Eliminating Dept. of Education, and Reducing Student Debt.** After successfully funding the development of the COVID-19 vaccinations, Donald Trump did a flip flop on vaccinations and embraced conspiracy theories about immunization. He now says his next Administration will cut off *all* federal funding from local schools if they require any vaccinations prior to enrollment—even though it is the law in all 50 states. Trump also proposes scrapping the *entire* Department of Education, which supplements school funding across the nation, and without which, local taxes would have to increase.[3] Trump also opposes the Biden-Harris Administration's student debt relief initiatives. *(Section 8—read time: 15 minutes.)*

9. **Abortion and the Values of Life, Liberty, Privacy, and Religious Freedom:** Donald Trump takes credit for overturning *Roe v. Wade*, which guaranteed individual freedom of choice on abortion during the first trimester. As a result, state legislators are now permitted to decide for individual Americans the

profoundly private, religious, and ethical questions regarding abortion. Trump and J.D. Vance want to go even further and *ban abortion nationwide*. Harris supports legislation that would restore *Roe v. Wade* and the right of women to have access to abortion up to viability, without government interference. *(Section 9—read time: 12 minutes.)*

10. **Overall Crime is Down, but Mass Shootings with Assault Weapons are Stoking Fear:** While overall crime has decreased in America over the last three decades, Americans *feel* less safe due to mass shootings. Mass shootings declined when America had a 10-year ban on military-style assault weapons; and there is evidence that renewing the ban would stop many of the mass shootings. Kamala Harris and Tim Walz (a veteran and hunter) want to renew the ban; Donald Trump will block renewal, continuing the mass shooting carnage. *(Section 10—read time: 9 minutes.)*

11. **Defense and Global Stability—Alliances v. Isolationism:** Donald Trump's first term brought us global instability—a trade war with China that raised prices; a failed attempt to rein in North Korea's nuclear missile development; a broken international agreement that has brought Iran much closer to possessing nuclear weapons; and repudiation of the NATO treaty that has kept the peace in Europe for 75 years. By contrast, the Biden-Harris Administration has skillfully protected the independence of Ukraine while avoiding a U.S.-European war with Russia by strengthening the NATO alliance; and has contained Chinese and North Korean expansionism by building new Indo-Pacific alliances. *(Section 11—read time: 9 minutes.)*

12. **Respecting Servicemembers and Veterans:** Donald Trump has mocked American soldiers who gave their lives and limbs in the service of our country as "losers" and "suckers"—comments he is now running away from. By contrast, in 2022, the Biden-Harris Administration signed and began implementation

of the bipartisan PACT Act, the most significant expansion of benefits and services for veterans in more than 30 years. *(Section 12—read time: 6 minutes.)*

13. **Climate—Escalating Floods, Wildfires, Droughts, and Violent Weather:** We can all see with our own eyes the rapidly escalating effects of global warming on America—increased flooding, droughts and out-of-control wildfires, stifling heat, and violent storms. The Biden-Harris Administration enacted the largest ever U.S. investment in clean energy and greenhouse gas reduction to slow climate change. Another Trump Administration would reverse course, cutting funding for clean energy technologies and again withdraw the U.S. from global climate agreements, condemning America and the world to a dystopic future of fires, floods, droughts, deadly heat, mass migrations and conflict. *(Section 13—read time: 9 minutes.)*

14. **Infrastructure, Competitiveness, and Energy Independence:** In his first term, Donald Trump *repeatedly promised* infrastructure investments but delivered *nothing.* The Biden-Harris Administration enacted the largest *bipartisan* investment in infrastructure in U.S. history, as well as unprecedented subsidies to rebuild the domestic computer chip industry. Energy independence has also increased under the Biden-Harris Administration. *(Section 14—read time: 9 minutes.)*

15. **Poverty, hunger, homelessness, and disability programs:** The Trump Administration tried to cut healthcare and nutrition programs for millions of Americans and tried to limit overtime pay for 8 million workers. Trump publicly mocks disabled people and calls poor people "morons." The Biden-Harris Administration enacted the American Rescue Plan Act which led to the lowest child poverty rate in American history, added one million people to Medicaid, and helped over 8 million renters stay in their homes during the pandemic. Harris proposes

extension and expansion of the child tax credit. *(Section 15— read time: 6 minutes.)*

16. **Americans want good leadership, which requires: (1) bipartisanship, (2) upholding the Constitution and the rule of law, and (3) appointing agency heads with experience and high ethical standards.** Donald Trump's signature legislation in his first term was a *partisan* tax bill unnecessarily cutting taxes for wealthy Americans while exploding the public debt by 50%; he presided over the longest federal government shutdown in history because he was *unable to negotiate annual spending bills*; and he blocked the most significant bipartisan immigration deal in nearly 40 years. Donald Trump's personal disrespect for the Constitution and the rule of law is unprecedented in U.S. history and, in 2019, *Bloomberg News* reported that, as President, he "surrounded himself with family members, appointees and advisers... accused of conflicts of interest... and violating ethics rules."[4] The Biden-Harris Administration has signed into law five major bipartisan bills and put in place strict ethical requirements for their appointees. *(Section 16—read time: 12 minutes.)*

CONCLUSION: *(read time: 5 minutes)*

ABOUT THE AUTHOR: From One Independent Voter to Another *(read time: 5 minutes)*

A NOTE ON "PROJECT 2025:" You will hear a lot this fall about extremist proposals in the Heritage Foundation's *Project 2025: Mandate for Leadership, The Conservative Promise.*[5] The Heritage Foundation is a right-wing think tank in Washington D.C. which initiated "Project 2025," a 900-page playbook for a second Trump term.

I have not addressed specifics of *Project 2025* in this book because Donald Trump is claiming not to know anything about it (although CNN research found that 140 people who worked on the project had served in the Trump Administration[6]). It is unnecessary for this book to address Donald Trump's knowledge of, or agreement with, *Project 2025* since his first term actions and recent statements give us a very clear picture of what to expect in a second Trump term.

§ 1. POLLS: AMERICANS REMAIN UNITED ON CORE VALUES

(Read Time: 10 minutes)

Politicians thrive on extreme speech and hyperbole to draw stark contrasts between themselves and their opponents. This is not new; it is an entirely natural component of an open society with free elections.

However, the Internet—especially social media and partisan media outlets—have supercharged the *perception of* deep divisions in America and have fueled the misperception that Americans are hopelessly divided.

There are also those who have attempted to use the July 13 assassination attempt to feed their message of division. Do not be distracted by the lone act of one deranged criminal.[7]

Polls in 2024 show that solid majorities of Americans continue to share core values, and the divisions are not nearly as deep, widespread, or dire as politicians, social media loudmouths, and Hollywood would like you to believe.

Set aside for a moment the "America is hopelessly divided" hysteria and the flood of nonsensical campaign ads and consider the following poll results on the core values shared by overwhelming majorities of Americans in 2024.

1

(1) Equal Protection Under the Law; Trial by Jury

Large majorities of Americans value the right to equal protection under the law—the belief that all people should be treated equally in the eyes of the law. A recent nonpartisan AP-NORC poll (conducted by the Associated Press and University of Chicago) reports that **91%** of U.S. adults say the right to equal protection under the law is extremely or very important to the United States' identity as a nation.[8]

Equal protection under the laws began as an aspiration in our Declaration of Independence "that all men are created equal...." In the same year, 1776, Thomas Paine made clear in his brilliant pamphlet, *Common Sense*, that this fundamental human equality is guaranteed by the rejection of absolute rule by kings and authoritarians in favor of the rule of law: "(I)n America the law is king.... and there ought to be no other."[9]

It took nearly a century of political turmoil culminating in the Civil War for this aspiration to move closer to reality with adoption of the Fourteenth Amendment in 1868, which prevents any state from "deny[ing] to any person...the equal protection of the laws."

It took nearly another century for the Supreme Court to declare that "separate educational facilities are inherently unequal;"[10] another decade for enactment of the Civil Rights and Voting Rights Acts to outlaw discrimination and guarantee the right to vote; several more decades for fulfillment of gender equality; and the full meaning of "equal protection" in our daily lives continues to evolve.

Despite robust national debate over the exact meaning of "equal protection," the broad national commitment to equal protection under the law, for all persons, continues to be strong and was perfectly stated in Martin Luther King Jr.'s aspiration that one day all will be judged "by the content of their character."[11]

Closely related to Americans' commitment to equal protection under the law is our shared commitment to **trial by jury.** A nonpartisan poll in 2022[12] found that **84%** of respondents share the common value that trial by jury ensures that "courts and judges only make decisions based on the Constitution, the law, and the facts of each case." Jury trials are the surest guarantors that every individual receives the equal protection of the laws, and today's juries are more carefully selected than ever with full input from prosecutors and defense teams.

The right to a jury trial has deep roots in American history. The Declaration of Independence cites the right to a jury trial as a fundamental right—rebuking King George III "for depriving us, in many Cases, of the Benefits of Trial by Jury." Thomas Jefferson once remarked that the right to a jury trial is even more important than representative government: "Were I called upon to decide, whether the people had best be omitted in the legislative or judiciary department, I would say it is better to leave them out of the legislative. The execution of the law is more important than the making of them."[13]

The dedication of the Founders to trial by jury is enshrined in the Bill of Rights. The Sixth Amendment provides that "In all criminal prosecutions, the accused shall enjoy the right to a speedy and public trial, by an impartial jury...." and for non-criminal (civil) cases, the Seventh Amendment likewise requires "trial by jury."[14]

This shared commitment of the American public to equal protection under the law, secured by the Constitution and the right to a jury trial, remains a fundamental protection against a government unjustly depriving any citizen of their life, liberty, or property.

(2) The Right to Vote

Nearly all Americans value the right to vote. The AP-NORC poll found that **91%** of U.S. adults say the right to vote is extremely or very important to the United States' identity as a nation.[15]

The right to vote has been a core American principle from the very beginning of migration to North America in the early 1600s. It is an accident of history that the early colonists found themselves over three thousand miles and several months sea travel from the British and other colonizing governments—thereby making self-government a necessity. But so it began, and the early colonies quickly became accustomed to, and protective of, self-government.

So ingrained became this core value of self-government among the rapidly growing colonies, that "no taxation without representation" became a central rallying cry of the movement for independence from the British crown. The right to, and importance of, self-government is recorded for posterity in our Declaration of Independence where Thomas Jefferson's brilliant words highlight the "Right of Representation in the Legislature" and rebuke King George III for "imposing Taxes on us without our Consent" and for "having dissolved Representative Houses repeatedly."[16]

Similar to "equal protection under the law," the right to vote began as an aspiration, but was not fully secured for all Americans until much later in our history: the Fifteenth Amendment in 1870 extended voting rights to black men (although poll taxes, literacy tests and grandfather clauses suppressed black voting rights for another century); the Nineteenth Amendment secured women's suffrage in 1920; the Indian Citizenship Act of 1924 granted the right to vote to Native Americans; in 1943, the Chinese Exclusion Act was repealed; in 1961, citizens of the District of Columbia were granted the right to vote for President (but still lack full representation in Congress); in 1964, the Twenty-Fourth Amendment banned poll taxes; in 1965, the Voting Right Act banned literacy tests and grandfather clauses; in 1971, Vietnam era draftees and all 18-year-olds secured the right to vote; in 1975, amendments to the Voting Rights Act enabled the rights of non-English speaking voters; and, in 1984, polling places were required to be accessible for people with disabilities and the elderly.

This continuous ambition, throughout American history, to make suffrage more universal reflects the right to vote as a shared value and a privilege that belongs to American citizens.

(3) The Freedoms of Speech, Press, and Assembly

Large majorities of Americans value the freedoms of speech, press, and assembly. The AP-NORC poll found that **90%** of U.S. adults say freedom of speech is extremely or very important to the United States' identity as a nation; **83%** say the right of the people to assemble peaceably (demonstrate) is extremely or very important; and a strong majority, **77%**, say freedom of the press is extremely or very important.[17]

Bolstering these results is a 2024 Pew Research Poll showing that more than **90%** of registered voters believe it is important to have public discussions of our nation's historical successes and its shortcomings.[18]

These rights are enshrined beautifully for all future generations of Americans in the first sentence of the First Amendment to our Constitution: "Congress shall make no law…abridging the freedom of speech, or of the press; or the right of the people peaceably to assemble…."

These three rights are intertwined. The right to speak freely exists only if people can express their views in peaceful assembly and can freely publish their views in newspapers, books, and other media.

To be sure, these rights are not absolute; courts have ruled that a person can be barred from screaming "fire" in a crowded theatre in order to protect life and limb; and governments can regulate the time, place, and manner of public assemblies and demonstrations to ensure they are peaceable and do not interfere with the freedoms of their fellow citizens.

Nevertheless, the rights to freely speak one's mind on all manner of subjects, to assemble with others for peaceable demonstrations, and to publish and disseminate one's views for all to read are core values shared by large majorities of Americans and are three of the pillars of American democracy.

(4) Freedom of Religion without Government Interference

Large majorities of Americans value freedom of religion without government interference. The AP-NORC poll found that **84%** of U.S. adults say freedom of religion is extremely or very important to the United States' identity as a nation.[19]

The centrality of freedom of religion is enshrined in the first words of the First Amendment: "Congress shall make no law respecting an establishment of religion, or prohibiting the free exercise thereof."

In a world where religious extremism frequently fuels intolerance, violence, and war, **America remains exceptional in its religious diversity,** the freedom to exercise one's chosen faith (or secular philosophy), and the separation of church and state that has allowed America's diverse religious and secular groups to flourish side-by-side.[20]

This adherence to the free exercise of religion, and rejection of government-established religion, can be traced back to America's earliest colonial days when Europeans suffering from religious persecution sought refuge in America. Thomas Paine, in *Common Sense*, reminded his fellow Americans in 1776 that "(t)his new world hath been the asylum for the persecuted lovers of civil and religious liberty from every part of Europe." Paine went on to suggest a constitution for the new nation "securing freedom and property to all… and above all things, the free exercise of religion, according to the dictates of conscience."

This commonly shared value was stated with exceptional eloquence in President George Washington's letter of August 18, 1790, to a religious congregation in Rhode Island:

> The Citizens of the United States of America have a right to applaud themselves for having given to mankind examples of an enlarged and liberal policy: a policy worthy of imitation. All possess alike liberty of conscience…. It is now no more that toleration is spoken of, as if it was by the indulgence of one class of people, that another enjoyed the exercise of their inherent natural rights. For happily the Government of the United States, which gives to bigotry no sanction, to persecution no assistance, requires only that they who live under its protection should demean themselves as good citizens….[21]

Americans will not tolerate interference with their own free exercise of religion, nor will they tolerate government establishment of one religion over another. Freedom of religion has been in our national DNA since our founding.

(5) The Right to Privacy Without Government Intrusion

Large majorities of Americans value the right to privacy without government intrusion. The AP-NORC poll reports that **90%** of U.S. adults say the right to privacy is extremely or very important to the United States' identity as a nation.

The beginnings of this shared value can be detected as far back as the Declaration of Independence with its emphasis on the "unalienable Rights… [to] Life, Liberty and the pursuit of Happiness" without "any Form of Government becom[ing] destructive of these ends…." In other words, our American Founders shared a common appreciation of the importance of making one's own life decisions without government interference.

The proper role and extent of public laws and regulations have been, and always will be, the source of vigorous debate at every level of government, but the commitment to privacy, itself, is a fundamental value shared by nearly all Americans.

This visceral American commitment to privacy eventually became manifest in constitutional law when the Supreme Court recognized a right to privacy in 1965, with Justice Douglas finding a privacy right derived, or implied from, several other rights set forth in the Bill of Rights—the right of association, the protection of persons, papers, and effects from government searches, the bar against quartering soldiers in private homes, and the guarantee against compelling individuals to provide evidence against themselves.[22]

While the constitutional right to privacy, as it relates to decisions on abortion, has now been rejected by the Supreme Court, the general right to privacy remains a strongly held value shared by the vast majority of Americans. (For a nonpartisan discussion of abortion, the recent *Dobbs* decision, and the policies likely to be pursued by the presidential candidates, see §9, below.)

(6) Economic Opportunity and the American Dream

Large majorities of Americans value economic opportunity. The AP-NORC poll reports that about **8 in 10 U.S. adults** believe "the ability of people living in the U.S. to get good jobs and achieve the American dream" is extremely or very important to the country's identity. Put another way, 80% of Americans believe the opportunity to be part of America's middle class is a core value.

Academics and policy wonks will argue endlessly about what income levels qualify as middle class; and liberals and conservatives will argue about the best ways to ensure that Americans have opportunities to join the middle class and whether government enhances or interferes with those opportunities.

Some believe government's role should be limited to ensuring opportunity by preventing *intentional discrimination*, while others believe government should play a more activist role in redressing *the effects of past discrimination* through measures aimed at equal outcomes. This will be an ongoing, and entirely natural, debate as we work towards a more perfect Union.

But there is no doubt that **the opportunity to work hard—free of discrimination—to earn a place in America's middle class is a shared value that transcends current divisions.**

(7) Conclusion

This section has highlighted that a solid majority of Americans continue to share common values – the right to equal protection under the laws; the right to vote for a representative government; the freedoms of speech, press and assembly; the right to freedom of religion without government interference; the right to privacy without government intrusion; and the opportunity to earn a place in America's middle class.

Instead of recognizing these shared values that have endured in America for a quarter of a millennium, extremist politicians and partisan media companies have sought to sow discord and division by peddling misinformation and fearmongering, and cynically labeling states—and people—as "red" or "blue." Such labeling demeans the American ideal that all people should be judged without prejudice and by the content of their character.

§ 2. THE ECONOMY:
The Facts about Inflation, Jobs, Taxes, and Public Debt

Introduction to Key Issues in America in 2024

*In 2024, the demagogues and dividers are spreading misinforma-
tion about the strength of our economy; immigrants; Social Security
and Medicare; healthcare and housing; education; abortion; crime;
America's defense; veterans; climate change; U.S. energy independence; poverty; and how to ensure the stability of our democracy
and institutions.*

*The following short sections unpack each of these issues in a non-
partisan, common-sense manner; address the misinformation spread
by political extremists, social media, and campaign ads; and lay out
the key decisions a Trump or Harris Administration are likely to
make in 2025, and beyond, to address each of these issues. Each fact
presented in this book is drawn from reputable, nonpartisan sources
and is clearly referenced and hyperlinked in the endnotes.*

The Economy: Inflation, Jobs, and Public Debt

(Estimated read time: 27 minutes)

Gallup reported in March of 2024 that "inflation" (prices increase
year-over-year) topped the list of Americans' concerns, with 55%
worrying a great deal about inflation, 52% worrying a great deal
about "the economy" in general, and 51% worrying a great deal
about "federal spending and the budget deficit."[23]

The U.S. economy is now in far better shape than these polls indicate. In fact, the U.S. has the strongest economy in the world. **Unemployment is low,** [24] **inflation has dropped to normal levels,**[25] **and economic growth has been steady**[26]—**with interest rate reductions by the Federal Reserve likely to begin in September 2024.**[27]

Public debt, though, remains a problem. The accumulated public debt and accompanying interest payments are growing faster than the economy, which is not sustainable.

The question for independent voters is which candidate for President will pursue policies to keep inflation down and the economy growing, while avoiding policies that will deepen the public debt.

To answer this question, the following are helpful facts from *nonpartisan, evidence-based sources* (which you can quickly access, if you wish, through internet links in the endnotes).

1. *Fact: Unemployment is at historic lows, and new manufacturing jobs have surged.*

   - Average unemployment during the Biden-Harris term is **4.1%, a near 50-year low.**[28] (A slight up-tik in July to 4.3%,[29] while still very low by historical standards, is leading the Federal Reserve to lower interest rates in September.)

   - During Donald Trump's term (including the pandemic downturn) the **economy lost 2.9 million jobs overall.**[30] Trump's average unemployment rate was **6.3%.**[31]

   - During the Biden-Harris Administration, the economy has added 15.7 million jobs overall—**6.3 million higher than before the pandemic.**[32]

   - Trump gives lip service to manufacturing jobs—and continues to—but when he left office, there were **178,000 fewer people employed in manufacturing.**[33]

- The Biden-Harris Administration has *added* **762,000 manu-facturing jobs**.[34] Due to federal investments in semiconductors, "companies are spending billions building factories in Arizona, Ohio, Upstate New York and Texas."[35]

2. *Fact: The U.S. today has the world's strongest economy.*

- The rebound of the U.S. economy from the Pandemic Recession of 2020 has been nothing short of remarkable. Thanks to three major COVID-19 relief packages enacted in in 2020 and the American Rescue Plan Act (ARPA) enacted in 2021, **the "Pandemic Recession" was one of the shortest on record,** with contraction in the economy lasting only two months—March to April of 2020.[36] By 2021, the economy (GDP) was out of recession and growth surged to 5.5%,[37] with growth continuing in 2022,[38] and reaching a robust 3.1% in 2023,[39] and **continuing strong growth at 2.8% in the second quarter of 2024.**[40]

- A report by the World Bank in June 2024 said, "the U.S. economy, in particular, has shown impressive resilience" and **credits the U.S. economy for driving growth in the global economy.**[41]

- During the Biden-Harris Administration, new business creation has surged to its "highest levels in decades."[42]

3. *Fact: Inflation is down, with the Federal Reserve indicating interest rate reductions will begin in September.*

Inflation (rising prices) happens when there is an imbalance between supply and demand. We all understand from personal experience that when there is a shortage of goods or services, without a drop in demand, prices increase. This is what caused inflation to spike in 2021.

The global COVID-19 pandemic severely disrupted global supply chains.[43] At the same time, the Trump and Biden Administrations, together with Congress, enacted several trillion dollars of economic relief to help America's businesses and families weather the economic storm, which propped up consumer demand.[44] With supplies down, and demand propped up, prices inevitably increased; by December 2021, inflation reached 7%.[45]

Inflation was exacerbated in 2022, with Russia's unprovoked invasion of Ukraine, which increased global energy prices (because Russia is a major energy exporter[46]) *and* increased food prices (because Ukraine is a major food exporter[47]). In March 2022, inflation topped 8%,[48] prompting the Federal Reserve to raise interest rates to tamp down demand and reduce inflation. (For a short nonpartisan explanation of how that works, see *How does the Federal Reserve affect inflation and employment,* linked in this endnote.[49])

After a series of interest rate hikes by the Federal Reserve, by June 2023, demand cooled down and inflation had dropped to 3.0%.[50]

A year later, on August 23, 2024, Federal Reserve Chair Jerome Powell said "inflation is on a sustainable path back to 2 percent," paving the way for likely interest rate reductions to begin in September 2024.[51]

While prices have now stabilized, Americans understandably are still feeling the effects of *cumulative price increases* from mid-2021 to mid-2023—the "inflation hangover."

Because we thankfully live in a free market economy, the government seldom attempts to mandate prices. The most recent attempts to do this during the Nixon Administration (a short-lived wage and price freeze) and the Carter Administration (windfall profits tax) were failures.[52]

The best prescription for addressing the inflation hangover is **avoiding any federal policies that could trigger renewed inflation.** Unfortunately, several recent proposals by Donald Trump are likely to trigger more inflation:

- **Trump's large tariffs would trigger inflation and job losses.**

  - Background: The individual income tax is the federal government's largest source of revenue. The income tax is applied to income in seven brackets, from 10% applied to income of $11,600 or less, up to 37% for income over $609,350.[53]

  - Trump proposes replacing income tax revenue with a 10% to 20% across-the-board tariff on imported goods[54] and a 60% tariff on all imports from China.[55] Tariffs are "largely passed on to consumers" as higher prices,[56] hitting those with low- and middle-incomes the hardest.

  - These huge tariffs would trigger an "inflationary burst" which would also slow business activity and kill an estimated 675,000 jobs.[57]

- **Trump's expulsion of millions would trigger inflation and job losses.**

  - Trump's proposed mass expulsion of 11 million-plus undocumented immigrants—in addition to the devastating implications for families and communities—would be devastating for the U.S. economy.[58]

  - It would abruptly remove millions of workers from the economy, surging the cost of labor for U.S. businesses. This would trigger inflation (higher prices) and likely cause an economic slowdown (recession). Economists call

the combination of inflation and recession "stagflation"—
which has not occurred since the 1970s. But prepare for it
if Trump imposes tariffs and expels millions of workers.

- **Harris seeks strict antitrust enforcement against "Big
Food" mergers that boost prices.**

  ◦ The Biden-Harris Administration does not support Trump's
  huge tariff increases or mass expulsions (see §3 below).

  ◦ Harris believes that "extreme consolidation in the food
  industry has led to higher prices that account for a large
  part of higher grocery bills." To confront that, she will
  "direct her Administration to crack down on unfair mergers and acquisitions that give big food corporations the
  power to jack up food and grocery prices and undermine…
  competition."[59]

4. Fact: Public Debt is dangerously high. Trump proposals would make the debt far worse; Harris proposals, less so.

Despite low inflation, low unemployment, strong and steady growth,
and a strong stock market, a major economic concern is that the federal "debt-held-by-the-public" will soon be larger than the economy,
which is not sustainable over the long-term.

As explained below, Donald Trump's proposals would seriously
exacerbate an already dangerous debt; Kamala Harris' policies pose
less danger.

Brief background on the Public Debt: When Congress enacts
more in spending authority for a year than Treasury collects in revenues, **annual "deficits"** result. The additional Treasury borrowing to finance that deficit adds to the **accumulated "public debt."**
Following four years of budget surpluses under President Clinton,

the government has run annual deficits every year since FY 2002—when the Bush tax cuts went into effect without budgetary offsets to pay for them.

Annual deficits since FY 2002 ballooned with:

(1) The 2001 and 2003 **Bush tax cuts** and later the 2017 **Trump tax cuts**—neither of which were paid for by spending cuts or offsetting revenue increases.[60]

(2) Expensive military operations in **Iraq and Afghanistan,** costing trillions,[61] (and a terrible loss of life—nearly a half million military and civilian deaths[62]).

(3) Trillions spent to stabilize the economy during the **Great Recession** (2007-09)[63] and the **COVID-19** pandemic (2020-23)—the latter being far more expensive.[64]

(4) Rapid increases in **Medicare** and **Social Security** spending due to retirement of the baby boomers, growing heath care costs, and addition of the Medicare Part D prescription drug benefit.[65]

(5) **Growing interest payments** on the accumulated public debt due to (i) the escalating size of the debt and (ii) the Federal Reserve's interest rate increases in 2022 and 2023 to tame inflation.[66]

Most public debt is held outside the government by individuals, financial institutions, and governments, and is called **"debt-held-by-the-public,"** which in August 2024 topped $28 trillion.[67]

Debt-held-by-the-public, as a percent of the economy (GDP),[68] grew from 34% in 2000, to 61% in 2010, 73% in 2015, 79% in 2019, and 99.8 % in 2020—a level it has remained close to for the last four years.[69]

Fact: Trump and Biden-Harris Records on the Debt: Donald Trump increased debt-held-by-the-public by **50%** during his first term.[70] The Biden-Harris Administration increased debt held by the public by **28.5%** as of July 2024.[71]

How Much Debt is Too Much?—Many on the political right and the political left have, at various times, argued that the size of annual deficits or the accumulated public debt does not harm the economy—although with different respective motivations.

On the political right, advocates for large tax cuts have argued that deficits do not matter, or that tax cuts will spur so much growth they will fully pay for themselves—a claim for which there is no evidence.[72] Tax cuts lose revenue and increase the debt unless offset by revenue increases or spending cuts.

On the political left, advocates for federal entitlement programs often dismiss the relevance of growing deficits, fearing it could build support for entitlement reforms which would mean smaller annual cost of living adjustments in benefits or loss of current benefits.[73]

The reality is that no one knows how much debt is too much. In 2010, a well-respected bipartisan debt reduction commission co-chaired by former Senate Republican Budget Chairman Pete V. Domenici (NM) and Democratic economist Alice Rivlin (Founding Director of the Congressional Budget Office, Budget Director in the Clinton White House, and Vice-Chair of the Federal Reserve Board) set 60% of GDP (Gross Domestic Product) as a reasonable goal for their bipartisan debt reduction plan based on a review of economic history.[74]

However, debt-held-by-the-public is now way beyond 60% of GDP—estimated to exceed 100% of GDP next year (2025).[75]

For several decades, fiscal responsibility advocates on both sides of the aisle have been warning that the U.S. must avoid a **"fiscal death**

spiral"—a scenario where larger and larger amounts are being borrowed each year simply to pay interest on a ballooning debt.

The U.S. has now arrived at that dangerous point. Interest payments on debt held by the public will reach $1 trillion in 2026.[76] Without meaningful changes in current federal spending and tax laws, interest payments are projected by the nonpartisan Congressional Budget Office to rise to **one-sixth of federal spending within a decade,**[77] **nearly one-fifth of spending within two decades, and nearly one-quarter of all federal spending within three decades**[78]— undermining America's ability to meet our defense and domestic priorities.

In dollar terms, debt-held-by-the-public will top $50 trillion by 2034, nearly twice what it was last year, and the government will spend more than 40% of all individual income taxes on interest payments on the debt.[79] These are current projections—**without extending the 2017 tax cuts** (many of which are expiring at the end of 2025), which would add *another* **$4.6 trillion** to the debt if not offset by spending cuts or revenue increases.

Due to the precarious debt outlook, two of the three major credit rating agencies (Standard & Poor's and Fitch) have downgraded U.S. government debt from the highest rating of AAA to AA+.[80]

What needs to happen? Common sense suggests:

(1) **"Do No Harm." Avoid making the situation worse** with unnecessary spending increases or tax cuts that are not paid for with offsetting spending cuts or revenue increases.

(2) **Gradually phase in a bipartisan package of spending restraints and new revenues** that, together, reduce annual deficits to sustainable levels where we are no longer in a feedback loop of borrowing ever-increasing amounts each year to make annual interest payments on the debt.[81]

Neither candidate has come forward with a long-term plan to stabilize the public debt. However, the two candidates are quite different with respect to whether they would avoid making current debt projections worse. In general, Donald Trump has made several proposals that would *seriously* worsen the debt; Harris' proposals would do less to exacerbate the debt.

- **Trump's economic plans would add at least another $7 trillion to the debt.**

  - **Background on Expiring Tax Cuts:** The nonpartisan Congressional Budget Office estimated that revenue losses from President Trump's 2017 tax cuts (known as "TCJA"[82]) added nearly **$1.9 trillion** to the public debt over 10 years.[83] While Trump's corporate tax rate cuts were permanent, the individual tax provisions of the 2017 tax law, as well as estate and gift tax breaks, and certain business tax breaks, will **expire at the end of 2025**.[84]

  - Donald Trump now proposes to extend *all* the 2017 tax cuts expiring in 2025,[85] without any budgetary offsets, which would **add nearly $4.6 trillion to the public debt** over 10 years[86]—and promises more tax cuts on top of the extensions.[87] (The highest-income households—roughly the top 5% of earners—would receive nearly half of the new tax cuts.[88])

  - Trump would further exacerbate the debt by ending taxation of Social Security benefits, **increasing the debt by another $1.6 to $1.8 trillion** through 2035.[89]

  - Trump would further exacerbate the debt by reducing the corporate income tax rate from 21% to 15%, **increasing the debt by another $700 to $910 billion** over 10 years.[90]

○ Trump would further exacerbate the debt by exempting tips from income taxes *and* payroll taxes, **increasing the debt by another $150 to $250 billion** over 10 years.[91]

• **Harris' economic plans would add significantly less to the public debt.**

○ Kamala Harris' position on extension of the 2017 tax cuts would **avoid the full $4.6 trillion debt increase** in two ways: (1) tax cut extensions would be **limited** to people earning under $400,000; [92] and (2) the costs would be **offset** by raising taxes on high-income earners and increasing the corporate tax rate from 21% to 28%.[93] The corporate rate increase would reduce deficits by $1 trillion over 10 years.[94]

   ▪ The Harris-Walz Aug. 16, 2024, policy release states their "commitment to fiscal responsibility, including by asking the wealthiest Americans and largest corporations to pay their fair share—steps that will allow us to make necessary investments in the middle class, while also reducing the deficit and strengthening our fiscal health." [95]

○ Harris has made several **additional tax proposals.** Whether they would increase the debt, and by how much, would depend on whether they are coupled with offsetting revenue raisers or spending cuts, and whether they are temporary or permanent. (Click on the endnote to link to an analysis of the costs before budgetary offsets are applied.[96])

   ▪ Harris would exempt tips from income taxes, increasing the debt by **$100 to $200 billion** over 10 years, unless the cost is offset.[97]

   ▪ Harris would restore and make permanent the 2021 American Rescue Plan's temporary **expansion of the**

child tax credit to $3,600 (up from $2,000) and would add a **new child tax credit** of up to $6,000 for lower- and middle-income families with children in their first year of life when expenses are highest.[98]

▪ Harris would restore the 2021 American Rescue Plan's **enhancement of the earned income tax credit (EITC)** which increased the maximum credit for workers without dependent children to roughly $1,500.[99]

▪ Harris would extend the 2021 American Rescue Plan's **enhanced Affordable Care Act health insurance subsidies** currently set to expire at the end of 2025 (delivered through the tax code).[100]

▪ Harris proposes a new tax incentive for "homebuilders who build starter homes sold to first-time homebuyers," and a new tax credit up to $25,000 for a downpayment for first-time home buyers.[101]

5. *Serious Risk: Trump's Election Could Trigger a U.S. Treasury Default*

• One of the earliest fiscal decisions Trump or Harris will face is how to avoid another debt limit crisis in 2025. In June 2023, the Biden-Harris Administration and then Republican Speaker Kevin McCarthy (R-CA) negotiated the *bipartisan* Fiscal Responsibility Act which placed caps on discretionary spending and extended the statutory limit on the public debt to January 2025.[102]

• Failure to raise the debt limit in 2025 would leave Treasury with insufficient cash to make payments on Treasury bonds; pay U.S. troops; make federal benefit payments to retirees, Medicare providers, and veterans; or fulfill financial obligations to states for hospitals, teachers, and contractors building roads, airports, and other essential infrastructure.

- Donald Trump said in 2023, **the U.S. "might as well" default on its debt**—his exact words—**perhaps the most fiscally irresponsible words ever spoken by a former President.**[103] A U.S. Treasury default on the nation's legally binding financial obligations would destroy the U.S. Treasury's credit rating, spike interest rates, trigger hyper-inflation, and lead to a severe recession and massive job losses.

Conclusion: Trump Proposals Would Trigger Inflation, Recession, Global Trade War

- **Donald Trump's proposals would cause economic chaos.** More than $7 trillion in new tax cuts—without offsets— would **explode the public debt** and burden the economy with unmanageable annual interest payments. Massive tariff increases and mass expulsions of undocumented immigrants would **trigger hyper-inflation,** and push the economy into a **recession, kill jobs**, and trigger a **global trade war** with profound **economic instability**. Trump's reckless attitude on a U.S. Treasury default could trigger an economic crisis from which the country could not recover.

- **Kamala Harris' economic policies largely follow the economic policies of the Biden-Harris Administration** which have brought us strong and steady growth since the pandemic, the lowest unemployment in nearly 50 years, millions of new jobs with a resurgence in U.S. manufacturing jobs, and during the last year, a return to stable prices and low inflation. Harris would extend the expiring 2017 tax cuts in a fiscally responsible manner by limiting the extensions to people earning under $400,000 and offsetting the costs with increased revenues from corporations and the wealthiest taxpayers.

- **16 Nobel-winning economists issued a warning in June 2024 about the risks to the U.S. economy of a second Trump presidency:**

  "Many Americans are concerned about inflation, which has come down remarkably fast. **There is rightly a worry that Donald Trump will reignite this inflation, with his fiscally irresponsible budgets.** Nonpartisan researchers... predict that if Donald Trump successfully enacts his agenda, it will increase inflation...

  The outcome of this election will have economic repercussions for years, and possibly decades, to come. We believe that a second Trump term would have a negative impact on the U.S.'s economic standing in the world and a destabilizing effect on the U.S.'s domestic economy" (emphasis added).[104]

- Final Note: I have devoted much of my professional life to developing fiscally responsible federal spending and tax policies for both Republicans and Democrats. In the Senate, and later at the White House Office of Management and Budget, I worked to advance legislation that brought about four years of U.S. budget surpluses. **Whatever preconceptions you may have about which political party would better manage the economy, I urge you to discard those notions.** In this particular election, with these two candidates, there is no question that **Donald Trump offers economic chaos, more inflation, and more debt**, while Harris offers stable prices and continuing economic stability.

§ 3: IMMIGRATION:
The Nonpartisan Facts

(read time: 24 minutes)

1. Americans' Anxiety about Immigration

Gallup reported in March 2024, "Amid the heightened numbers of migrants entering the United States at the Southern border and discord in the Middle East, Americans have grown more anxious about immigration… over the past year…. For the second straight month, immigration leads Americans' unprompted answers about what most ails the nation…" According to the poll, 48% of Americans worry about illegal immigration a great deal.[105]

Sorting through the noise and extremist claims: Is today's immigration actually the huge problem some politicians are claiming, or is the current wave of immigration similar to prior waves of immigration, which brought your ancestors to America? Here are the facts.

2. The Immigration Pendulum: Vacillating between Welcoming and Exclusion

America is a nation of immigrants. The first immigrants crossed a narrow strip of land from Asia to what is now Alaska thousands of years ago and migrated south, becoming Native Americans. Millennia later, after Christopher Columbus brought news of America to Europe in the 1490s, communities of European immigrants began to colonize the Eastern seaboard in the early 1600s, including the British in New England and Virginia, the Dutch in New York, the Spanish in Florida, and the Swedes in Delaware. Some made the perilous sea journey seeking religious freedom, and others seeking economic opportunity on a resource-rich continent. Others, unfortunately, arrived against their will from Africa and would not secure freedom and opportunity until centuries later.

Despite America being a nation of immigrants, attitudes towards *new* immigrants, by those who came before, have swung like a pendulum, vacillating between welcoming and exclusionary, reflecting the unfortunate and persistent human frailty to fear people who are different.

The swing of the immigration pendulum is reflected in the brief timeline below: [106]

- **In 1790,** the English were the largest ethnic group among the white population, while nearly one-fifth of the total population were of African heritage.

- **A major wave of Irish and German immigrants occurred between 1820 and 1860.** A backlash against Irish immigrants led, in 1849, to the establishment of America's first anti-immigrant "populist" party, the so-called "Know-Nothing Party." Like the MAGA populist movement today, Know-Nothing leaders "claimed to speak for ordinary people, taking an us-versus-them stance," and using anti-immigrant rhetoric, conspiracy theories, and religious discrimination to stir up anger against outsiders.

- **Beginning in the 1850s a steady flow of Chinese immigrants began** building railroads, seeking work in gold mines and garment factories, and filling agricultural jobs. This led to passage of the Chinese Exclusion Act in 1882,[107] barring Chinese immigrants. Although they made up only 0.002% of the U.S. population, Chinese immigrants were blamed for depressing wages.

- **A major wave of Italian and Jewish immigration occurred between 1880 and 1920** seeking jobs and opportunities in America's rapid period of industrialization and urbanization. An influx of **Japanese workers** also occurred during this period. With an estimated three-quarters of New York City's population in 1910 consisting of new immigrants and "first-generation Americans,"[108] anti-immigrant xenophobia reached new heights by the start of World War I.

- **Backlash Closes the Doors:** The **Immigration Act of 1917** established a literacy requirement for immigrants entering the country which stopped immigration from most Asian countries.[109] The **Immigration Act of 1924**[110] severely limited the number of immigrants through national origin quotas. The formula severely impacted immigration of Italians and Jews from Southern and Eastern Europe and completely barred Asian immigration (except from the Philippines).

- **The Doors Open Again:** In 1948, the first refugee and resettlement law opened the door to Europeans seeking to immigrate in the wake of World War II and the Holocaust.[111]

- **In 1952, the Immigration and Nationality Act (INA)**[112] ended the exclusion of Asian immigrants.

- **1956-57:** The U.S. admitted 38,000 **Cold War refugees** after the failed Hungarian uprising against the Soviet Union. In all, over three million refugees were admitted during the Cold War.

- **1960-62:** 14,000 unaccompanied children were admitted from Castro's Cuba.

- **In 1965, the INA was amended to** end the 1924 national origin quotas, replacing it with a 7-category preference system **emphasizing family reunification and skilled workers.**

This was followed by increased immigration from war-torn regions of Asia including Vietnam and Cambodia.

- In 1980, the "Mariel boatlift" saw 125,000 Cubans crossed the Straits of Florida seeking political asylum.

- In 1986, President Ronald Reagan signed the Simpson-Mazzoli Act,[113] granting amnesty to nearly three million undocumented immigrants in the U.S., and going forward, required employers to check the legal status of all potential employees.

- After 1986, despite the Simpson-Mazzoli requirement that employers check immigration status, the undocumented immigrant population increased due *primarily* to people who arrive in the U.S. legally but overstay their visas, and *secondarily*, people who arrive without visas and claim asylum due to persecution in their native countries. "About 8.3 million U.S. workers in 2022 were unauthorized immigrants." The total unauthorized immigrant population in the U.S. stands at about 11 million, *below* the peak of 12.2 million in 2007.[114] Claims of 15 or 20 million undocumented immigrants and hysterical language about an "invasion" are baseless.

- In March 2021, monthly apprehensions of undocumented migrants at the U.S. Mexico border began to increase markedly due to migrants claiming asylum and, later on, the end of COVID-19 restrictions.[115]

- In early 2024, in response to the increase, Administration and Senate negotiators agreed on bipartisan border security legislation that would have significantly tightened the requirements for asylum, allowed closing of the border when border crossings reach high daily levels, and increased funding for border officers and expediting the asylum review process. However, at the urging of former President Trump, Senate

Republicans reversed course and blocked passage of the bipartisan border security package in February 2024,[116] and again in May 2024.[117]

- **Summer 2024—Southern Border Crisis Contained:** With defeat of the bipartisan border package, the Biden-Harris Administration issued in early June 2024 an executive order permitting the closing of the southern border when migrant crossings reach high daily levels.[118] As of July 2024, unlawful border crossings reached the lowest level since September 2020.[119]

3. How the Immigration System Works—A Quick Overview[120]

The openness of America to persons of all ethnicities is reflected in "birthright citizenship," the constitutional guarantee enshrined in the Fourteenth Amendment after the abolition of slavery, that any person born within the territory of the U.S. is a citizen, regardless of the citizenship of one's parents.

Federal law (the Immigration and Nationality Act or "INA") provides four basic pathways to U.S. immigration: (1) family reunification, (2) employment, (3) a lottery to promote country-of-origin diversity, and (4) humanitarian immigration (fleeing persecution). In 2021, 740,000 individuals were granted legal permanent residency through the four pathways below. In late 2022, more than four million applicants were on the State Department's waiting list for family-related and employer-related visas.[121] Following is the breakdown of total immigration by category:

(1) Family Reunification (58%).[122]

- The law sets no limit on the admission of spouses, unmarried minor children, and parents of U.S. citizens.

- Other family members (siblings and adult children) may apply for a limited number of visas under a "family preference system."[123]

(2) Employment-Based Immigration (27%):[124]

- *Permanent* employment-based immigration is capped at 140,000 per year divided into five preference categories (extraordinary ability, professions, skilled workers, former U.S. government employees, and entrepreneurs aiming to set up businesses).

- *Temporary* employment-based visa classifications permit employers to hire foreign nationals for specific jobs for limited periods. These include more than 20 visa classifications varying by eligibility requirements, duration, and whether workers can bring dependents.

(3) Humanitarian Immigration:

- **Refugees (3%)**[125] are admitted to the U.S. based upon an inability to return to their home countries because of a **"well-founded fear of persecution" due to their race, politics, religion, or national origin.** Each year, the President, in consultation with Congress, determines the ceiling for refugee admissions which are allocated by region. In addition: *Humanitarian Parole Authority* allows people to enter the U.S. *temporarily* for urgent humanitarian reasons even though they may not qualify for refugee status; *Temporary Protected Status (TPS)* is granted to people in the U.S. who cannot return home because of a natural disaster or armed conflict; and *Deferred Enforced Departure*, allows protection from deportation for people whose home country is unstable.

- **Asylum (5%)**[126] is available to persons *already in the U.S.* who are seeking protections for the same reasons as refugees, i.e., a "well-founded fear of persecution." This includes undocumented migrants who have been apprehended at the border and released pending an asylum hearing.

(4) **Country-of-origin Diversity Lottery (4%)**:[127] The Diversity Visa Program was created by the Immigration Act of 1990 for immigrants from countries with low rates of immigration (subject to a cap of 50,000) who have either a high school education or two years working in a profession. Diversity visas have generally benefitted immigrants from African and Eastern European countries.[128]

Per-Country Ceilings: "Under the per-country cap set in the Immigration Act of 1990, no country can receive more than 7% of total employment-based and family-sponsored preference visas in a given year."[129]

Lawful Permanent Resident and a Pathway to Citizenship: Once a person obtains an immigrant visa, they become a Lawful Permanent Resident ("LPR" or Green Card Holder) and can remain in the country without limitation. An individual who has had LPR status for at least 5 years (or three in some cases) may apply for citizenship if they are at least 18, demonstrate continuous residency and good moral character, pass English and U.S. history and civics exams, and pay an application fee.[130]

Non-Immigrant Visas for temporary workers, tourists, and students: Each year, the U.S. also grants *non*-immigrant visas to numerous categories of temporary workers (subject to annual caps), and well as tourists and students (without caps). These non-immigrant visas can last for multiple years and may in some cases lead to becoming a lawful permanent resident. "In FY 2022, the U.S. granted 206,000 visas for high-skilled workers, known as H1B visas, and more than 298,000 visas for temporary workers in agriculture and other industries, or H2A visas."[131]

Deferred Action for Childhood Arrivals (DACA) was established in 2012 for people who were brought to the U.S. illegally as children, through no fault of their own, permitting them to remain in the U.S. for at least two years as long as they have no criminal record and have a diploma. It does **not** provide a pathway to legal status and requires renewal.[132]

4. *Correcting Immigration Misinformation*[133]

More than any other issue in America today, the facts about immigration have been lost in a morass of political misinformation, fearmongering, and extremist rhetoric. Following are key facts on the most prevalent immigration myths from nonpartisan, reliable sources.[134]

- **Immigration is not a drag on the economy; it grows the economy:** In 2024, the nonpartisan Congressional Budget Office projected "the higher growth rate of… GDP over the next five years stems mainly from rapid growth in the labor force, reflecting a surge in the rate of net immigration from 2022 to 2026 compared with recent years." [135] Moreover, immigrants made up nearly one-fifth of the U.S. civilian workforce in 2022.[136]

- **Only U.S. citizens are permitted to vote.** There is no evidence of noncitizens attempting to vote, despite fraudulent claims by Donald Trump of "millions of people who voted illegally." We are all aware from personal experience how carefully our voter registration information is checked and double-checked when we go to the polls to vote.

- **Undocumented Immigrants do not burden the U.S. budget.** The opposite is true; immigration can improve the fiscal solvency of Social Security and Medicare, the two biggest challenges in the U.S. budget. Undocumented immigrants are ***not*** eligible for benefits from federal programs.[137] Moreover, immigrants can actually improve the U.S. fiscal picture. Social

Security and Medicare Hospital Insurance are both projected to become insolvent in the next decade due to the aging of our population, with more retirees collecting benefits and fewer workers sending payroll taxes to the Treasury. Immigration is one common sense way to help solve this problem, because immigrants tend to be young and go right into the workforce. According to the Congressional Budget Office, a "large proportion of recent and projected immigrants are expected to be 25 to 54 years old—adults in their prime working years."[138]

- **Undocumented immigrants are *not* committing more crimes than people born in the U.S.** A recent nonpartisan study found that "relative to undocumented immigrants, U.S.-born citizens are over 2 times more likely to be arrested for violent crimes, 2.5 times more likely to be arrested for drug crimes, and over 4 times more likely to be arrested for property crimes" (emphasis added).[139]

- **Most fentanyl entering the U.S. is *not* being smuggled by undocumented migrants seeking asylum.** The U.S. *does* have a serious fentanyl and drug abuse problem; however, it is *not* due to undocumented migrants illegally crossing the southern border seeking asylum. According to the nonpartisan Congressional Research Service, most fentanyl and other illegal drugs are being smuggled into the U.S. at official ports of entry.[140] The solution is to increase customs inspections at ports of entry and that requires more funding from Congress.

- **America is not "full." Expelling undocumented migrants and shutting our doors to new immigrants would seriously damage our economy, causing inflation and recession, and cause Social Security and Medicare to go broke sooner.** America has one of the lower population densities in the world. (Population density measures the average number of people per square mile.) Of the 250 countries and territories in the world, the United States has one of the lower population densities, in the bottom third, at #187.[141] Moreover, if we were to shut our doors to new immigrants and expel all undocumented immigrants, it would close businesses for lack of workers, increase inflation due to the higher costs of scarce labor, send the U.S. economy into recession due to business closures and inflation, and accelerate the projected insolvency dates for Social Security and Medicare due to the worsening imbalance of workers to retirees.

5. *Eleven Million Undocumented Immigrants Living in the U.S.*

In 2024, the U.S. has an estimated 11 million undocumented immigrants, due *primarily* to people who arrive in the U.S. legally but overstay their visas, and *secondarily*, people who arrive without visas and claim asylum due to persecution in their native countries. The latter are released into the U.S. to await asylum determinations which can take years because Congress has underfunded the immigration court system, with more than two million cases currently pending.[142]

The last time the issue of undocumented immigrants was addressed was in 1986, when President Reagan signed the Immigration Reform and Control Act, which made it illegal for employers to hire undocumented immigrants but granted legal permanent status for 2.7 million people. Upon signing the act at the Statue of Liberty, Reagan said, "The legalization provisions in this act will go far to improve the lives of a class of individuals who now must hide in the shadows, without access to many of the benefits of a free and open society. Very soon many of these men and women will be able to step into the sunlight and, ultimately, if they choose, they may become Americans."[143]

- **Donald Trump** has called for **mass deportations** of undocumented immigrants using national guard or the military[144]— **separating families**, **damaging the economy** by abruptly removing workers from businesses across the country, triggering **inflation** by raising the cost of scarce labor, **accelerating the insolvency of Social Security and Medicare** by reducing payroll tax receipts, and violating federal laws prohibiting the use of military force inside the country.[145]

- **The Biden-Harris Administration has proposed** allowing undocumented immigrants to apply for temporary legal status, with the ability to apply for green cards (legal permanent residence) after 5 years **if they pass criminal and national security background checks** and pay their taxes; and resources would be increased to address the backlog.[146] This approach would **keep families together, boost the economy** by enabling more workers to fill open jobs, and improve the solvency of Social Security and Medicare by boosting payroll tax collection. In 2024, nearly **60% of registered voters** said that undocumented immigrants currently living in the U.S. should be allowed to stay in the country legally.[147]

6.   *Undocumented Migrants Crossing the Southern Border*

In early 2024, the Biden-Harris Administration supported Senate bipartisan legislation to significantly reduce the number of undocumented migrants crossing the southern border; it would have given the President emergency authority to restrict border crossings if they reach unmanageable daily levels, tightened requirements for granting asylum, and provided more budgetary resources to clear out the backlog of pending asylum claims.[148]

- **Donald Trump** urged Senate Republicans to oppose the bipartisan reforms—in order to keep alive the "immigration issue" on which he has been campaigning since 2015,[149] instead of solving the problem.[150]

- **Kamala Harris** has committed to signing the bipartisan agreement.[151]

- After Donald Trump supporters blocked the bipartisan deal, the Biden-Harris Administration issued an **executive order** in June 2024 permitting the closure of the southern border when migrant crossings reach high daily levels, although funds to clear the administrative backlog are still required.[152] As of July 2024, unlawful border crossings have reached the lowest level since September 2020.[153]

7. *Young People Brought to the U.S. without Documents When They Were Children*

- **The Biden-Harris Administration** has urged Congress to pass the American Dream and Promise Act to permit as many as 2.3 million young people brought to the U.S. as children, through no fault of their own, an opportunity to obtain permanent legal status provided they have a high school diploma or are in the process of completing one *and* pass background checks.[154]

- **Donald Trump**, while President, attempted to terminate DACA (which protects young people from deportation), but he was blocked by the Supreme Court in 2020.[155]

8. *Refugee Admissions into the U.S.*

Providing a safe haven for people fleeing persecution has been a fundamental pillar of U.S. immigration policy since World War II, reversing the anti-immigrant laws of the 1920s which forced masses to perish in Europe under Hitler's genocide because they had nowhere to go. The U.S. passed its first refugee legislation in the wake of WWII and accepted refugees fleeing communist regimes throughout the Cold War. The President sets annual caps on refugee admissions.[156] In 2023, the largest numbers of refugees fleeing persecution came from Congo, Syria, Afghanistan, and Myanmar.

- **Donald Trump,** as President, pushed the annual cap on refugees to a record low of 15,000 for 2021.[157]

- **The Biden-Harris Administration** revised the cap to 62,500 in their first year in office, setting it at 125,000 for each subsequent year, although about 61,000 were admitted in 2023.[158]

9. *General Attitudes on Immigrants and Discrimination*

- **Donald Trump:** On December 16, 2023, at a rally in New Hampshire, Donald Trump said illegal immigrants and migrants from "all over the world," like South America, Africa, and Asia, are "poisoning the blood of our country."[159] Trump then repeated the use of "poisoning" in a social media post, saying in an all-caps post, that "illegal immigration is poisoning the blood of our nation. They're coming from prisons, from mental institutions — from all over the world," a debunked lie.[160] The term **"blood poisoning" was used by the Nazi dictator Adolph Hitler** in his racist and anti-Semitic manifesto *Mein Kampf*, in which he blamed Germany's economic problems on the mixing of races.[161]

- **Biden-Harris:** "Joe Biden decided to run for President after what we all saw in Charlottesville in 2017, when Neo-Nazis marched from the shadows spewing the same antisemitic bile that was heard in Europe in the 1930s."[162] On January 26, 2021, the Biden-Harris Administration announced initiatives to promote fair housing policies, strengthen relationships with Native Americans and Alaska Natives, and combat discrimination against Asian Americans and Pacific Islanders.[163] On May 25, 2023, Biden released the first-ever U.S. National Strategy to Counter Antisemitism.[164]

§ 4: MIDDLE CLASS RELIEF:
Housing, Child Care, Student Loans, and Medical Debt

(Read time: 12 minutes)

A recent poll reports that about **8 in 10 U.S. adults** believe "the ability of people living in the U.S. to get good jobs and achieve the American dream" is extremely or very important to the country's identity.[165] Put another way, 80% of Americans believe the opportunity to be part of America's middle class is a core value.

The middle class today faces a number of challenges, especially young families affording their first house and childcare costs, and middle-class Americans burdened with the hangover effects of inflation on food prices, as well as student loans and medical debt.

Following are the Harris and Trump records and policies that would impact the middle class.

Harris Record and Policies Impacting the Middle Class

- **Millions More Jobs:** The Biden-Harris economy has added 15.7 million jobs,[166] added 762,000 manufacturing jobs,[167] and has racked up the lowest unemployment rate in nearly 50 years.[168] In addition, historic new investments in infrastructure and domestic manufacturing of computer chips are generating good-paying new jobs across the country. (see §14).

- **Inflation Brought Under Control:** The COVID-19 pandemic and Russia's invasion of Ukraine triggered inflation in 2021 and 2022 (see §2), but prices stabilized in record time and the Federal Reserve is now poised to begin reducing interest rates in September 2024.[169]

- **Tax Relief for the Middle Class:** Harris will extend lower tax rates for the middle class when they expire at the end of 2025.[170]

- **Restore and Expand the Child Tax Credit:** Harris would restore and make permanent the 2021 American Rescue Plan's temporary expansion of the child tax credit to $3,600 (up from $2,000) and would add a new child tax credit of up to $6,000 for lower- and middle-income families with children in their first year of life when expenses are highest.[171]

- **Relief on Health Insurance Premiums:** The Biden-Harris Administration passed the American Rescue Plan Act (ARPA), which temporarily expanded eligibility for, and increased, ACA health insurance subsidies. These were extended by the Inflation Reduction Act (IRA) through 2025. Harris proposes to make the expanded subsidies permanent.[172]

- **Assistance for First-Time Home Buyers:** Harris proposes a new tax incentive for "homebuilders who build starter homes sold to first-time homebuyers," and a new tax credit up to $25,000 for a downpayment for first-time home buyers.[173]

- **Slow the Increases in Home and Rental Prices:** Harris would slow the increase in home prices with legislation to stop Wall Street investors from buying up homes in bulk and raising prices ("buying up and marking up");[174] and would slow the increase in rental prices with legislation to stop rent-setting data firms from price fixing.[175]

- **Extend the Solvency of Social Security:** Low- and middle-income seniors rely heavily on Social Security benefits. The Biden-Harris Administration has proposed extending Social Security solvency by applying the 12.4% payroll tax (half paid by employers and half by workers) to income above $400,000.

- **Extend the Solvency of Medicare:** Low- and middle-income seniors rely heavily on Medicare benefits. To extend the solvency of the Medicare Hospital Insurance Trust Fund, the Biden-Harris Administration has proposed directing revenues from the Net Investment Income Tax into the Trust Fund.[176]

- **Hold Down Prescription Drug Prices:** To reduce costs for millions of Medicare beneficiaries, the Biden-Harris Administration (in the Inflation Reduction Act ["IRA"] of 2022) capped out-of-pocket spending for prescription drugs at $2000/year beginning in 2025.[177] The IRA also capped monthly insulin prices for all Medicare beneficiaries at $35. Harris has proposed extending Medicare's $35 insulin cap and the $2,000 annual cap on out-of-pocket drug expenses, to all insurance plans.[178]

- **Medical Debt Relief:** In 2024, the Biden-Harris Administration announced a proposed rule to remove medical debt from credit reports of 15 million Americans.[179] Harris would go further, saying she will "work with states to cancel medical debt for millions of Americans."[180]

- **Student Loan Debt Relief:** While focusing on the two major efforts at broad-based student debt relief (up to $20,000), the Biden-Harris Administration has also sought to improve access to existing debt relief programs for students who have been defrauded by their schools, or who work in the nonprofit or public sectors, or are disabled.[181] In May 2024, the Department of Education said that "more than one out of every 10 federal student loan borrowers has now been approved for some debt relief"—nearly 5 million borrowers and $167 billion in debt relief.[182]

• **Reducing Child Care Costs:** On February 29, 2024, Vice President Harris announced actions to lower child care costs for more than 100,000 families, including: capping co-payments for families participating in the child care & development block grant program to no more than 7% of income; encouraging states to eliminate co-payments entirely for families of children with disabilities, children experiencing homelessness, children in foster care, children in Head Start, and families at or below 150% of the federal poverty level; and directing states to pay childcare providers more fairly and on time to improve financial stability for 140,000 child care providers and incentivizing more providers to enter the program.

• **Worker Protections:** United Farm Workers President Teresa Romero credited Vice President Harris for pushing through heat protections for outdoor workers.[183]

Trump Record and Policies Impacting the Middle Class

• **Job Losses:** During Trump's presidency, there were 178,000 **job losses in manufacturing.**[184]

• **Tax Relief that Explodes the Debt:** Trump would extend all of the tax cuts expiring at the end of 2025.[185] This includes tax relief for the middle class, but also includes large cuts for the wealthiest Americans—without budgetary offsets—exploding the public debt by $4.6 trillion. According to an analysis released in July 2024, more than 45% of Trump's extension of the expiring tax cuts would go to the highest income households.[186]

- **Trigger Hyper-Inflation:** Trump would replace income taxes with **huge tariffs**[187] **on imported goods**—that would immediately be passed along to consumers as higher prices[188] and likely trigger recession and job losses.[189] In addition, Trump's mass expulsion of millions of immigrants[190] would surge the cost of labor, **triggering even more inflation.** Sixteen Nobel Laureates in economics have warned that Trump will trigger renewed inflation.[191]

- **Cause Social Security and Medicare Trust Funds to Go Bankrupt Sooner:** Low- and middle-income seniors rely heavily on Social Security and Medicare benefits. Trump has proposed no specific measures to extend the solvency of the Social Security or Medicare Trust Funds but has promised actions that would cause the Social Security and Medicare Trust Funds to go bankrupt sooner.[192] On July 31, 2024, Trump proposed eliminating the partial taxation of Social Security benefits,[193] which would advance Social Security's insolvency date to 2032, and the Medicare HI Trust Fund insolvency date by six years to 2030.[194] Trump has also promised mass deportations of undocumented immigrants[195] living in the United States who pay billions each year into the Trust Funds. By reducing payroll tax revenues, Trump's deportation plan would further advance the insolvency dates.

- **As President, Trump tried to Repeal the Affordable Care Act Which Has Helped Millions of Low- and Middle-Income Americans Access Health Coverage:** The ACA provides affordable health insurance premiums to millions of low- and middle-income Americans, as well as guaranteeing coverage for people with preexisting conditions and long-term acute diseases, and young people starting out. As President, Donald Trump promised to repeal and replace the ACA.[196] Every attempt to terminate it failed in Congress, and he never proposed a replacement.[197] Terminating the ACA would have caused 23 million Americans[198] to lose health coverage.

- **Opposed to Student Loan Debt Relief:** Donald Trump is staunchly opposed to student loan debt forgiveness. In June 2024, he called student loan debt forgiveness plans "vile" and, if elected, would almost certainly reverse course on the Biden-Harris efforts to provide permanent student loan debt forgiveness.[199]

§ 5: SOCIAL SECURITY:
Who Will Save Social Security?

(Read time: 5 minutes)

Social Security is a pillar of American society. Today over 66 million retirees and dependents, disabled workers and dependents, and survivors of deceased workers receive monthly Social Security benefits.[200]

Social Security is facing a serious long-term shortfall because declines in fertility and increasing lifespans are reducing the ratio of workers to retirees.[201] The 2024 Social Security Trustees Report[202] projects the Old-Age and Survivors Insurance (OASI) Trust Fund will be "solvent," i.e., able to pay all scheduled benefits, only until **2033.** At that time, the Fund's reserves will be depleted and ongoing income from the payroll tax will be sufficient to pay only 79% of scheduled benefits (or 75% if Trump's repeal of Social Security taxes goes into effect).[203]

At that time—in 2033—Congress will have the following options:

1. Borrow funds from the Disability Insurance Trust Fund to cover the OASI shortfall, but that would extend solvency only two more years, and then *both* trust funds would be insolvent by 2035.

2. Make up the shortfall with general revenues from the Treasury, but that would worsen the public debt.

3. Allow automatic reduction of benefit payments to 79% of scheduled benefits (or 75% if Trump's repeal of Social Security taxes goes into effect).[204]

45

Establish a New Bipartisan Commission

The better approach is to follow the example of the 1983 National Commission on Social Security Reform (informally known as the Greenspan-Moynihan-Dole Commission)[205] and set up a new bipartisan commission to develop a reasonable set of benefit, eligibility, and payroll tax reforms to guarantee the long-term solvency of the program. In order for this to be successful, it must happen soon, because reforms take time to phase in and "bend" the spending and revenue curves sufficiently to reach long-term solvency. For an example of one bipartisan plan that would have achieved long-term solvency, without raising the retirement age, see the 2010 Domenici-Rivlin plan, *Restoring America's Future.*[206]

Increasing Legal Immigration as a Partial Solution

One common sense means of improving the solvency of Social Security would be to increase legal immigration to the United States. Immigrants tend to be younger and of working age and would immediately increase the amount of payroll tax revenues supporting the Social Security system, as well as boosting the overall economy.[207]

Trump Positions on Social Security

- **Donald Trump** has proposed no specific measures to extend the solvency of Social Security but has promised actions that would **cause Social Security to go bankrupt sooner.**[208]

  - On July 31, 2024, Trump proposed eliminating the partial taxation of Social Security benefits,[209] which would advance Social Security's insolvency date by over one year to 2032 (as well as **increasing deficits by $1.6 trillion to $1.8 trillion** through 2035).[210]

- ○ Trump has also promised mass deportations of undocumented immigrants[211] living in the United States who pay each year into the Social Security Trust Funds. By reducing payroll tax revenues, Trump's deportation plan would further advance the insolvency date.

Harris Position on Social Security

- **The Biden-Harris Administration** has proposed extending Social Security solvency by applying the 12.4% payroll tax (half paid by employers and half by workers) to income above $400,000, leaving income *between* $168,800 (this year's wage cap) and $400,000 exempt from the tax.[212]

§ 6: HEALTHCARE: Protecting Medicare and Expanding Affordable Care

(Read Time: 18 minutes)

America has a patchwork quilt of healthcare coverage which depends on age, income, employment status, demography, and health status:

- **Employer-provided health plans** (covering about 55% of Americans).[213]

- **Medicaid** pays for healthcare for people near or below the federal poverty level, is financed jointly by the federal and state governments, and is administered by the states (covering about 19% of Americans).[214]

- **Medicare** is national health insurance for people ages 65 and older, disabled workers, and people with renal disease and ALS[215] (covering about 19% of Americans).[216]

- **The Children's Health Insurance Program (CHIP)** provides low-cost health coverage to children in families that earn too much money to qualify for Medicaid but not enough to purchase insurance on their own.[217]

- **The Affordable Care Act** subsidizes the purchase of private health insurance for people with modest incomes who are not eligible for Medicare, Medicaid, or CHIP.[218]

- **Veterans' Health Administration** hospitals and facilities provide direct healthcare to veterans with service-connected disabilities and/or low incomes.[219]

- **TRICARE** covers active-duty military, retirees, and immediate family members.[220]

- **CHAMPVA** covers dependents or survivors of a veteran who is permanently and totally disabled by a service-connected disability.[221]

- **Indian Health Service** facilities provide direct healthcare to American Indians and Alaska Natives.[222]

1. Protecting Medicare

There are two key issues facing Medicare's financial solvency: (1) the depletion of the Hospital Insurance Trust Fund in 2036; and (2) the escalating overall cost of the Medicare program, which is a major driver of the public debt.

Quick Backgrounder on Medicare

- **Medicare** is a **national health insurance program** established in 1965 which now covers 66 million older and disabled Americans (and people with renal disease and ALS).[223]

- The program is administered by the federal Centers for Medicare & Medicaid Services (CMS), which contracts with private companies for claims processing.

- Medicare has 4 parts:

  1. **Hospital Insurance (Medicare Part A)** covers the costs of hospital care, home health services following hospital

stays, skilled nursing facilities, and hospice care for all seniors and disabled workers who qualify. It is financed, through the HI Trust Fund, by HI payroll taxes and taxes on Social Security benefits. Part A is mandatory for seniors.

2. **Medicare Part B** covers doctor and outpatient services, including annual physicals, tests, physical therapy, diabetes care, medical equipment, and mental health services. Part B is optional.

3. **Medicare Part D** provides coverage for prescription (Prescription) drugs. Part D is optional.

4. **Medicare Advantage (Part C):** Traditional Medicare pays reimbursements for each fee or service. In an effort to contain the rapidly growing costs of traditional Medicare, the government launched an alternative, called "Medicare Advantage" which pays companies a specified amount per person per year to **bundle together all inpatient, outpatient, and prescription drug benefits**. Some Medicare Advantage plans also include dental and vision services. **Nearly half** of all Medicare beneficiaries now participate in Medicare Advantage.[224]

- **General federal revenues pay for about three-quarters** of Medicare Parts B, C, and D, with premiums covering the remainder.[225]

Medicare Hospital Insurance Trust Fund to be depleted by 2036

The HI Trust Fund supports Medicare's Hospital Insurance program (Part A). The Trust Fund receives about 90% of its financing from the HI portion of **payroll taxes**. Employees and their employers each pay 1.45% of total wages (and self-employed people pay an equivalent 2.9% of their self-employment income). Taxpayers with incomes over $200,000, for singles, and $250,000, for couples, pay an additional 0.9% of wages or self-employment income.[226] The remainder of the HI Trust Fund income is covered primarily by income taxes collected on Social Security benefits.[227]

The Medicare Board of Trustees estimates that the HI Trust Fund will run surpluses through 2029, followed by deficits thereafter until the trust fund becomes depleted in **2036**. In that year, Medicare would be able to pay **only 89% of costs** covered by Part A using payroll tax and other revenues.[228]

At that time, Congress could make up the shortfall with general revenues from the Treasury, but that would worsen the public debt. Alternatively, Congress could act before 2036 to extend the solvency of the Trust Fund through a combination of benefit changes and HI payroll tax increases.

Escalating Cost of Medicare Is a Major Driver of the Public Debt

Medicare has become one of the fastest growing programs in the federal budget—with a total cost of nearly $1.1 trillion—but the escalating costs of Parts B, C, and D seldom receive the attention they deserve because they are technically funded by the "Supplementary Medical Insurance Trust Fund," which automatically receives whatever funds it needs from general revenues. Nevertheless, the Medicare program, as a whole, is a major driver of the public debt—projected by the Congressional Budget Office to grow from an average of **2.6%** of GDP over the last 30 years, to **3.2%** in 2024 to **4.2%** in 2034, and **5.1%** in 2044—**at which point Medicare will cost more than all of defense and nondefense discretionary spending combined.**[229]

As explained above, the purpose of Medicare Advantage was to rein in the growth of Medicare costs. However, Medicare Advantage has **not** resolved the federal government's rapidly rising Medicare costs. The growing budgetary costs of Medicare, **due to the aging of the population and rising healthcare costs,** remains one of the main drivers of the escalating U.S. public debt.

Immigration as a Partial Solution to Medicare Solvency

Similar to Social Security, discussed above, one means of improving the solvency of the Medicare HI Trust Fund would be to increase legal immigration to the United States, and create a pathway to legal status for undocumented immigrants. Immigrants tend to be younger and of working age and would increase the amount of payroll tax revenues supporting the Hospital Insurance Trust Fund.[230]

Trump Positions on HI Trust Fund Solvency and Medicare

- **Donald Trump** has proposed no specific measures to extend the solvency of the Medicare Hospital Insurance Trust Fund but has promised actions that would **cause the HI Trust Fund to go bankrupt sooner.**

  - On July 31, 2024, Trump proposed eliminating the partial income taxation of Social Security benefits,[231] which would advance the Medicare HI Trust Fund's insolvency date by **six years,** to 2030, (as well as **increasing deficits by $1.6 trillion to $1.8 trillion** through 2035).[232]

  - Trump has also promised mass deportations of undocumented immigrants[233] living in the United States who have payroll taxes withheld for the Medicare HI Trust Fund. By reducing payroll tax revenues, Trump's deportation plan would further advance the insolvency date.

- ○ In addition, as President, Donald Trump sought numerous times to repeal the Affordable Care Act. That would have reduced payroll taxes on high earners, accelerating the financial insolvency of the HI Trust Fund.

- As President, Trump repealed the Independent Payment Advisory Board prior to its implementation due to conspiracy theories about "death panels" and "rationing of healthcare."[234] IPAB was designed to implement measures aimed at controlling overall Medicare costs.[235]

Harris Positions on HI Trust Fund Solvency and Medicare

- To reduce costs for millions of Medicare beneficiaries, the **Biden-Harris** Administration (in the Inflation Reduction Act of 2022, "IRA") **capped out-of-pocket** spending for prescription drugs at **$2,000/year** beginning in 2025.[236]

- The IRA also **capped monthly insulin prices** for all Medicare beneficiaries at **$35**. Harris proposes to extend the $35 cap to all insurance plans.[237]

- To extend the solvency of the HI Trust Fund, the Biden-Harris Administration has proposed directing revenues from the Net Investment Income Tax into the Trust Fund.[238]

- To reduce the overall costs of the Medicare program, the Biden-Harris Administration, in the Inflation Reduction Act of 2022, **gave Medicare authority to negotiate prices for some prescription drugs**—with the number growing over time—beginning with reductions of 40% to 80% for some drugs beginning in 2026. Harris wants to accelerate the timetable of negotiations.[239] The Inflation Reduction Act also requires that drug companies pay rebates when they increase prices faster than inflation.[240]

2. Affordable Care Act (ACA): The Facts

The ACA, often called "Obamacare," has been the object of endless partisan rhetoric and misinformation. These are the facts:

- **The Affordable Care Act** was enacted in March 2010[241] to close a large gap in U.S. healthcare, with millions of Americans lacking access to affordable health insurance. By 2013, the year before the major provisions of the ACA went into effect, more than 44 million individuals lacked coverage.[242] With enactment of the ACA, the uninsured share of the population had been nearly cut in half by 2016—the most significant expansion of health coverage since the enactment of Medicare and Medicaid in the 1960s.[243]

- **The ACA expanded access by:**

  - **Enabling states to expand Medicaid coverage (90% federally funded)** to people earning slightly above the federal poverty level (FPL);[244] and

  - **Providing subsidies to purchase private health insurance** for people with incomes between 100% and 400% of the Federal Poverty Level—who are not eligible for Medicare, Medicaid, or CHIP (Children's Health Insurance). In 2024, the 400% income eligibility cap is $60,240 for individuals and $124,800 for a family of four.[245]

- **The subsidies,** delivered as tax credits, are used to purchase private insurance through online health insurance "exchanges" established by the states, or through the federal exchange **(www.healthcare.gov)** for people in states that have not established an exchange. All insurance plans must provide "essential benefits," a requirement that enables enrollees to make apples-to-apples comparison of plans and to avoid plans that shortchange enrollees through benefit exclusions.

- **Protects people with pre-existing conditions:** The ACA prohibits insurance companies from denying coverage or charging higher premiums due to pre-existing conditions— one of the key reasons that people lacked coverage prior to the ACA.

- **Prohibits Lifetime Limits on Benefits:** The ACA prohibits insurance plans from capping lifetime coverage of essential benefits to protect people with chronic and acute health conditions.

- **Capped out-of-pocket costs:** All policies must provide an annual maximum out-of-pocket payment cap. After the cap is reached, all remaining costs are paid by the insurer.

- **No out-of-pocket costs for preventive care,** vaccinations, and medical screenings such as mammograms and colonoscopies.

- **Incentivizes for small employers to provide health insurance** with tax credits up to 50% of their employer's contribution.

- **Expanded coverage to young people by allowing adult children** to remain on their parents' plans *until* age 26.[246]

Trump Positions on the Affordable Care Act and Health Care

- **As President, Donald Trump** promised to repeal and replace the ACA.[247] Every attempt to terminate it failed in Congress, and he never proposed a replacement.[248] Terminating the ACA **would have caused 23 million Americans to become uninsured.**[249]

- Although he failed to repeal or replace the ACA, Trump took many actions as President to **weaken the ACA**:

Slashed the advertising budget 90%, leaving the public without information on the availability of insurance subsidies;[250]

Cut the beneficiary enrollment period in half;[251]

Cut funds for enrollment assistance;[252]

Stopped payments for cost-sharing subsidies[253] which increased premiums, deductibles, and out-of-pocket charges to low-income participants; [254] and

Supported a **failed court** challenge to have the ACA declared unconstitutional.[255]

Harris Positions on the Affordable Care Act and Health Care

- The Biden-Harris Administration reversed many of the steps Donald Trump took to weaken the ACA.[256] A record **45 million people now have coverage through ACA subsidies or Medicaid expansion.**[257]

- By the end of 2023, a *Morning Consult* poll of registered voters found that 57% approved of the ACA, including **56% of independents.**[258]

- The Biden-Harris Administration passed the American Rescue Plan Act (ARPA), which temporarily **expanded eligibility for, and increased, ACA health insurance subsidies.** These were extended by the Inflation Reduction Act (IRA) through 2025. Harris proposes to make the expanded subsidies permanent.[259]

- The Biden-Harris Administration enabled **dependents of families with unaffordable employer-based family coverage** to qualify for ACA health insurance subsidies.[260]

- Harris has proposed extending Medicare's **$35 insulin cap** and the **$2,000 annual cap on out-of-pocket drug expenses**, to all insurance plans.[261]

- The Biden-Harris Administration **beefed up staffing requirements for Medicare-certified nursing facilities**.[262]

- In 2024, the Biden-Harris Administration announced a proposed rule to **remove medical debt from credit reports** of 15 million Americans.[263] Harris would go further, saying she will "work with states to *cancel* medical debt for millions of Americans" (emphasis added).[264]

- **Global Cooperation:** The Biden-Harris Administration, recognizing the critical role of the World Health Organization in responding to global pandemics, reversed the Trump decision to withdraw from the WHO and restored U.S. funding.[265]

§ 7. HOUSING: Affordability for Renters and Buyers

(Read Time: 6 minutes)

Americans are concerned about the affordability of housing— for rentals and for purchase. A poll in May 2024 by the Bipartisan Policy Center, National Housing Conference, and Morning Consult, found that 74% of respondents believe the lack of affordable homes is a significant problem in the United States.[266]

The poll also found the concern about housing affordability cuts across party lines, with more than two-thirds of Independents, Democrats, and Republicans sharing the concern; and nearly half of renters and one-third of homeowners reported having difficulty paying their rent or mortgage payments over the past year.

Background on Current Housing Programs

Local governments control land use regulations and zoning that impact the supply of housing. However, since the U.S. Housing Act of 1937,[267] the federal government has put substantial federal resources into assisting low-income Americans with the affordability of housing:

- **Housing Choice Vouchers**—the largest federal housing assistance program—provides low-income Americans with subsidies to reduce monthly housing payments to an affordable percentage of monthly income, generally 30% to 40%. The subsidies can be used for apartments, townhomes, or single-family homes and are paid directly to the landlord, with the recipient paying the balance.[268]

- **Public housing programs** enable local housing agencies to receive federal grants to build and operate housing for low-income people at rents they can afford.[269]

- **Affordable housing in rural areas** is addressed through rental assistance, interest subsidies, grants, direct loans, and loan guarantees administered by the Department of Agriculture.[270]

- **Veterans may receive guaranteed home loans**[271] and homeless veterans may receive vouchers for monthly rent.[272]

- **In 2021, the Biden-Harris Administration created the Homeowner Assistance Fund**, authorized by the American Rescue Plan Act, providing nearly $10 billion to assist homeowners having difficulties with mortgage payments, insurance, and utility bills due to the COVID-19 pandemic.[273]

Harris-Walz Proposals Aimed at Lowering the Costs of Renting and Owning a Home

On August 16, 2024, the Harris-Walz campaign released a set of proposals aimed at addressing the housing shortage and addressing the rising costs of renting and owning a home: [274]

- **Tax incentives for homebuilders** to build "starter homes sold to first-time homebuyers."

- **Downpayment assistance for first-time homebuyers** with up to a $25,000 tax credit.

- **Incentivizes to build affordable rental housing** by expanding the Low-Income Housing Tax Credit.

- **A $40 billion fund** to incentivize innovative housing solutions at the local level.

- **Slow the increase in home prices** with legislation to stop wall street investors from buying up homes in bulk and raising prices ("buying up and marking up").

- **Slow the increase in rental prices** with legislation to stop rent-setting data firms from price fixing.

The Trump Record on Housing

- As President, Donald Trump proposed massive cuts to federal affordable housing programs for low-income Americans. [275]

- In his final budget submission, Trump proposed to slash the budget for the Department of Housing and Urban Development (HUD) by nearly $10 billion or 18% below the prior year's congressionally enacted levels.

- Trump proposed eliminating several programs, including funding to ensure "public housing agencies (PHAs) have money they need to address their most pressing capital needs, like fixing leaking roofs or replacing outdated heating systems."

- Trump also proposed increasing rents on some of the nation's poorest families who are recipients of the limited number of housing subsidies.

§ 8. EDUCATION: Grade School & Vaccinations, Eliminating Dept. of Education, Student Loan Debt Relief

(Read Time: 15 minutes)

K-12 Funding

This short subsection on K-12 education funding covers federal support for local schools together with vaccinations, because **Donald Trump has linked the two issues, saying he will cut off federal funding from local schools if they require vaccinations;** this, despite the reality that vaccinations are required by **state laws in all 50 states** prior to school enrollment in order to prevent the spread of dangerous childhood diseases.[276]

In addition, Trump has at various times pledged to **cut all federal education funding in half**[277] and **eliminate the Department of Education entirely.**[278]

Background on Federal Support for Local Schools

- Federal "Title I" grants provide **$18 billion** in operating assistance to local schools serving high concentrations of low-income students.[279]

- The federal government provides **$14 billion** in assistance to local schools for special education services for children with disabilities which only partially pays for the costs associated with Individual Education Plans required by the Individuals with Disabilities Education Act.[280]

- Education Department grants also support **rural** schools, instruction in English language, expansion of **charter** and **magnet** schools, and education services for **Indian, Native Hawaiian**, and **Alaska Native** students.

- Without these major infusions of federal education funding, local governments would be forced to raise local taxes.

Background on Vaccination Mandates

- In the 1850s, Massachusetts became the first state to mandate smallpox vaccination for school children.[281] In 1905, the Supreme Court ruled in *Jacobson v. Massachusetts* that states could enforce vaccination mandates.[282]

- By the early 1900s, nearly half of the states had vaccination requirements for children entering school and **by the early 1980s, all 50 states had vaccination laws** covering students first entering school.[283]

Correcting Myths About Vaccines

- "Immunization through vaccination is the safest way to protect against disease…. [V]accines produce an immune response similar to that produced by the natural infection, but without the serious risks of death or disability connected with natural infection."[284]

- "Deadly diseases that seem to have been all but eradicated have a… habit of making a come-back when immunization rates drop – as we see with the recent measles outbreaks across Europe. Only by making sure everyone gets their [shots] can we keep the lid permanently on vaccine-preventable diseases."

- "Giving several vaccines at the same time has no negative effect on a child's immune system."

- "There is no scientific evidence to link the MMR (Measles, Mumps, Rubella) vaccine with autism.... This unfortunate rumor started with a single 1998 study which was quickly found to be seriously flawed, and was retracted by the journal that published it."

- The COVID-19 mRNA (messenger ribonucleic acid) vaccines were not "rushed"; they were studied for decades "across a range of diseases, including flu, Zika and rabies [and] cancer. This type of vaccine delivers a set of instructions to the cells and teaches them to make a protein that produces an immune response to the virus."[285]

- "[H]igh vaccination coverage in a population reduces the spread of the virus, giving it fewer opportunities to mutate."[286]

- "None of the COVID-19 vaccines available in the U.S. use the live virus that causes COVID-19, and they cannot give you the disease or cause you to test positive."[287]

- "COVID-19 vaccines continue to protect against hospitalization and death."[288]

Trump Positions on Vaccinations

- **Donald Trump has flip flopped:** in his first term, Trump accelerated development of the COVID-19 vaccine with Operation Warp Speed (a success for his Administration),[289] but now has completely flipped—sensing political advantage in promoting false conspiracy theories about vaccines—and is threatening to eliminate funding for schools which have *any* vaccine requirements. Under a Trump-Vance Administration, schools would lose federal funding (including for low-income, rural, charter, and special needs students) if they maintain current state immunization requirements to prevent outbreaks of measles, polio, and other dangerous diseases.[290]

Biden-Harris Positions on Vaccinations

- **Biden-Harris Administration:** While the Trump Administration had put money into development of the COVID-19 vaccines, they had not put in place detailed plans for distribution—leaving it up to the states. The CEO of State and Territorial Health Officials praised the Biden-Harris Administration for "the unprecedented coordination between federal, state, local health authorities and pharmacy partners... resulting in 500 million COVID-19 vaccine doses administered in [the Biden-Harris Administration's] first year in office."[291]

- The Government Accountability Office reported on extensive use of the Defense Production Act to remediate medical supply shortages during the pandemic.[292] Further, recognizing that pandemic mitigation requires global cooperation, the Biden-Harris Administration resumed coordination with the World Health Organization, from which the United States had withdrawn during the Trump Administration, and donated hundreds of millions of vaccine doses to other countries to stem the global spread of Covid and blunt the emergence of new variants.

Trump and Harris Positions on Federal Funding of Education

- Donald Trump proposes **scrapping the Department of Education**, which supplements local school budgets across the nation. An abrupt end to federal education support would necessitate **local taxes increasing** throughout the country— although schools in rural and low-income urban areas would struggle to fill the funding gap due to their lower tax bases.[293]

- The Biden-Harris Administration's American Rescue Plan included the **largest single federal investment in education** to help schools compensate for the disruptions from the COVID-19 pandemic.[294]

- Harris supports increasing funding for K-12 to increase teacher pay[295] and supports federal funding for universal pre-K.[296]

Higher Education: Biden-Harris and Trump Positions on Student Loan Debt Relief

- Background: The Higher Education Act authorizes three types of student loans, amounting to $1.6 trillion, owed by 45 million borrowers; most of these are Direct Loans made by the Education Department.[297]

- During the pandemic, in March 2020, there was bipartisan agreement—starting in the **Trump Administration** and continuing into the **Biden-Harris Administration**—to put loan repayments *temporarily* on hold and pause accumulation of interest and collections to assist borrowers in coping with the economic fallout from COVID-19.[298] This temporary pandemic relief, enacted into law by the CARES Act,[299] remained available, through a series of extensions, until June 30, 2023.

- At almost the same time, in March 2020, Joe Biden, as a candidate for the Democratic nomination, said he would support *permanent* student loan debt relief of up to $10,000.[300]

- Following inauguration in 2021, the Biden-Harris Administration began developing plans for permanent student loan debt relief.

- On August 24, 2022, the **Biden-Harris Administration** announced the first **broad-based** student-loan debt forgiveness program—invoking a 2003 law (the HEROES Act)—to **permanently cancel up to $10,000 of federal student loans** (and up to **$20,000** for those receiving Pell grants). The Administration estimated up to 43 million borrowers would be eligible.

- However, in June 2023 the Supreme Court struck down the plan, ruling the policy exceeded the Administration's statutory authority under the 2003 HEROES Act.[301]

- Despite the setback on permanent debt relief, the Biden-Harris Administration in August 2023, launched the **SAVE** Plan—an **income-driven repayment plan** that calculates payments based on a borrower's income and family size—not their loan balance—and forgives remaining balances after a certain number of years. **Twenty million borrowers are estimated to be eligible**.[302] SAVE was to begin operating in July 2024, but is currently **on hold** pending two legal challenges.[303]

- On April 8, 2024, the Biden-Harris Administration announced a **second attempt at broad-based permanent student loan debt forgiveness** using different legal authority—"compromise and settlement" authority in the Higher Education Act—which it hopes will withstand legal challenge. The new plan—aimed at minority and community college borrowers—would cancel debt for borrowers who have experienced significant interest accrual and owe more than they did at the start of repayment, borrowers who first entered repayment more than 20 years ago, borrowers who attended failed schools, borrowers who qualify for existing forgiveness but haven't applied, and borrowers experiencing hardship.[304] The Department of Education began widely publicizing the new plan to 40 million borrowers on August 1, 2024.[305]

- While focusing on the two major efforts at broad-based student debt relief, the Biden-Harris Administration has also sought to **improve access to existing debt relief programs** for students who have been defrauded by their schools, or who work in the nonprofit or public sectors, or are disabled.[306] In May 2024, the Department of Education said that "more than one out of every 10 federal student loan borrowers has now been approved for some debt relief," or nearly 5 million borrowers and $167 billion in debt relief.[307]

- **Donald Trump is staunchly opposed to student loan debt forgiveness.** In June 2024, he called student loan debt forgiveness plans "vile" and, if elected, would almost certainly reverse course on the Biden-Harris efforts to provide permanent student loan debt forgiveness.[308]

§ 9. ABORTION and the Values of Life, Liberty, Privacy, and Religious Freedom

(Read Time: 12 minutes)

Democracy requires us to respect that good and decent people will sometimes disagree on matters of core convictions and the instruments of government must not be used to impose one set of beliefs on the entire nation.

As noted in Section 1 of this book, one of the values held in common by the vast majority of Americans is the **"right to privacy."** The AP-NORC poll reported that 90% of U.S. adults say the right to privacy is extremely or very important to the United States' identity as a nation.

In addition, the poll found that 84% of U.S. adults say **freedom of religion** is extremely or very important to the United States' identity as a nation. Moreover, the rights to **life and liberty** are enshrined as core American values at the beginning of our Declaration of Independence. Each of these values is relevant to the complicated issue of abortion.

Despite its complexity, Americans are not nearly as divided on abortion policy as extremist politicians would like you to believe. As explained below, a solid majority of Americans want to protect individuals from government interference in reproduction decisions in the first trimester of a pregnancy. The sad news is that self-serving, cynical politicians have been using the issue of abortion since the 1980s to drive a wedge between Americans for their own electoral advancement.

In this section, I offer an independent view that this issue is a mess because, in 1973, the Supreme Court failed to recognize that religious freedom is at the heart of this issue. **The question of when life begins (or when a human soul comes into existence) is an inherently religious question to be made according to one's own faith**. Politicians writing into law their own religious views on when human life begins is a clear violation of the First Amendment protection against establishment of religion.

Background: *Roe v. Wade* and *Casey*

Between 1967 and 1973, about one-third of states had enacted provisions permitting abortions in instances other than where the mother's life was in danger.[309]

In 1973, in the landmark case *Roe v. Wade*,[310] a pregnant woman brought a class action suit challenging the constitutionality of a Texas criminal abortion law which outlawed abortion except on medical advice for the purpose of saving the mother's life. The Supreme Court, in a 7-2 decision, ruled that the Texas law violated the Due Process Clause of the Fourteenth Amendment, which the Court interpreted as protecting a "right to privacy" which the Court majority interpreted as including a woman's right to terminate her pregnancy. While the Constitution does not explicitly reference a "right to privacy," the Court found that a right to privacy is implied from the Constitution's other protections of individual rights.[311]

The Court went on to rule:

- **in the first trimester of a pregnancy**, the abortion decision must be left to the woman and her physician without any state interference;[312]

- **in the second trimester of a pregnancy**, the decision remains private, but the state may regulate abortion procedures "in ways that are reasonably related to maternal health;"[313] and

- **in the third trimester of the pregnancy**, with the fetus reaching viability (able to survive outside the womb) the state may prohibit abortion except where "necessary...for the preservation of the life or health of the mother."[314]

The Court justified this three-trimester approach, explaining that it was weighing the state's interests in protecting the pregnant woman's privacy, health, and the "potentiality of human life," at various stages of the woman's approach to term.

In a related case, *Doe v. Bolton*, the Court further elaborated their ruling, finding a Georgia statute unconstitutional because its requirements for hospital accreditation, approval by a hospital abortion committee, and independent examinations all unduly burdened a woman's fundamental right to abortion.[315]

In the decades subsequent to *Roe* and *Doe*, there was litigation over the types of abortion requirements that did, or did not, unduly burden a woman's right to abortion.[316] In particular, in 1992, in *Planned Parenthood v. Casey*,[317] the Court (5-4) reaffirmed the constitutional right to have an abortion grounded in the liberty protected by the Fourteenth Amendment's Due Process Clause, and noted that the right to abortion is consistent with the Court's holdings protecting personal decisions relating to marriage, procreation, family relationships, child rearing and education, and contraception.[318]

The Court, in *Casey*, also underscored the importance of the legal principle that judges should respect settled law (a principle called *stare decisis*) and said "overruling Roe's central holding would not only reach an unjustifiable result under *stare decisis* principles, but would seriously weaken the Court's capacity to exercise the judicial power and to function as the Supreme Court of a Nation dedicated to the rule of law."[319]

Dobbs v. Jackson Women's Health Organization

Thirty years later, in 2022, in *Dobbs v. Jackson Women's Health Organization*,[320] in an abrupt reversal of settled law, the Court ruled 6-3 that the Fourteenth Amendment's Due Process Clause does *not* confer a right to abortion, *Roe* and *Casey* are overruled, and the states can resume regulating abortion without limitation.

The *Dobbs* Court rejected the importance of adhering to settled law when interpreting the Constitution—attempting to justify its action by making an analogy to the landmark *Brown v. Board of Education*[321] civil rights ruling in 1954 that overturned the infamous *Plessy v. Ferguson* ruling of 1896. *Plessy* had permitted "equal but separate accommodations for the white and colored races,"[322] which *Brown* overturned.

In writing the *Dobbs* decision, Justice Alito's attempt to rely on the *Brown* reversal of *Plessy* was a hollow argument since the *Brown* reversal was based on decades of facts on the ground demonstrating that "separate is inherently unequal," while the *Dobbs* decision had no changed set of facts on abortion upon which to reverse 50 years of settled law. The only circumstance that had changed was Donald Trump's very intentional appointment of three abortion foes to the Court—Justices Gorsuch, Kavanaugh, and Barrett.

The unfortunate ease with which the *Dobbs* Court overturned *Roe* was due to the weakness of the Court's legal reasoning in *Roe*. The Court in *Roe* should have acknowledged that the issue of abortion turns on *when human life begins*—a fundamental question of religious conviction that is protected from government interference by the First Amendment.

For people who believe human life begins at the moment of conception with the creation of a human soul, it is natural that abortion would be considered unacceptable as the taking of a human life. However, for people who believe that conception marks a beginning, which does not mature into human life until viability, abortion prior to viability is a private decision on reproductive healthcare and family planning.

Profound questions about when human life begins are the most fundamentally "religious" of all questions and, as such, should be fully protected from government intrusion and interference under the **First Amendment.**

Had *Roe* been decided on this basis—that the question of when human life begins is fundamentally religious and cannot be established by government—we might have avoided today's situation where these fundamental issues have been unwisely placed in the hands of state politicians.

Most importantly, as Americans, we should respect that reasonable, decent, and ethical people can arrive at entirely different conclusions about when human life begins, and respect that each person must make this decision consistent with their own religious faith—free from government establishment.

As a practical matter, a majority of Americans seem to agree with this general approach. Recent polling data from Gallup found that more than two-thirds of Americans (69%) believe abortion should remain a private matter of conscience in the first trimester and oppose state laws that would ban all abortions.[323]

A majority (60%) also *disagree* with the Supreme Court's decision to overturn 50 years of settled law under *Roe v. Wade.*[324]

Trump-Vance on Abortion

- **Donald Trump** appointed three justices to the Supreme Court (Neil Gorsuch, Brett Kavanaugh, and Amy Coney Barrett) with the expressed purpose of overturning *Roe v. Wade.* On

May 17, 2023, Donald Trump wrote, "After 50 years of failure, with nobody coming even close, I was able to kill *Roe v. Wade*."[325]

○ Trump has stated numerous times that he favors state politicians making decisions on abortion, [326] rather than protecting individual freedom to decide questions of religious faith and conscience.

○ On June 10, 2024, Trump said he walks "side by side" with a group saying abortion should be "eradicated."[327]

○ In 2022, J.D. Vance said he "would like abortion to be illegal nationally."[328]

○ Trump reinstated and expanded the "Mexico City" policy requiring foreign non-governmental organizations (NGOs) to certify they would not "perform or actively promote abortion as a method of family planning" using funds from *any* source as a condition of receiving U.S. family planning funding—an attempt to impose a minority religious view in the United States on donors to humanitarian programs around the world.[329]

Harris on abortion:

• **Kamala Harris** supports legislation that would restore *Roe v. Wade's* national standard of abortion legality up to viability and the right of women to make these decisions without government interference.[330]

• The Biden-Harris Administration issued guidance affirming that **abortions performed to stabilize the health of people experiencing pregnancy-related emergencies** are protected by the federal Emergency Medical Treatment and Active Labor Act (EMTALA).[331]

- The Biden-Harris Administration **rescinded Trump's "Mexico City" policy**, requiring foreign non-governmental organizations (NGOs) to certify they would not "perform or actively promote abortion as a method of family planning" using funds from *any* source as a condition of receiving U.S. family planning funding.[332]

§ 10. CRIME: Overall Crime Is Down, but Mass Shootings with Assault Weapons Stoke Fears

(Read Time: 9 minutes)

Crime and violence consistently rank among the top U.S. issues of concern, after immigration and the economy.[333] The Pew Research Center reported in April 2024 that "a growing share of Americans say reducing crime should be a top priority for the president and Congress to address this year. Around six-in-ten U.S. adults (58%) hold that view today, up from 47% at the beginning of Joe Biden's presidency in 2021."[334]

Here is the question, though: are Americans concerned about crime and violence because the incidents of crime and violence are actually increasing, *or* are the concerns increasing because 24-7 social media feeds are saturating our lives with images of mass shootings (one visible and heinous type of crime that has increased)?

Violent and Property Crimes in the U.S. Have *Decreased.*

Crime statistics come from two sources: the Federal Bureau of Investigation (FBI) publishes annual data on **crimes reported** to federal, state, and local law enforcement agencies, and the Bureau of Justice Statistics (BJS) **surveys Americans asking whether they were the victims of crime** in the past six months (which captures both reported *and* unreported crimes). Based on these two sources, here is what we know:

- Both the FBI and BJS data show **overall significant declines in U.S. violent and property crime rates since the early 1990s.** (These are national trends; particular types of crime in specific localities may have increased in particular years.) [335]

- FBI data shows **violent crime falling 49% between 1993 and 2022**, with overall decreases in robbery (down 74%), aggravated assault (down 39%) and murder/manslaughter (down 34%). [336]

- FBI data shows **property crime falling 59% between 1993 and 2022**, with large declines in burglary (down 75%), larceny/theft (down 54%) and car theft (down 53%). [337]

- Despite the overall decreases in violent and property crime rates since 1993, the national **homicide rate** increased in 2015 and again between 2019 and 2020 and remained up during the COVID-19 pandemic, although it came down in 2023, and remains significantly below the homicide levels of the early 1990s. [338]

Notably, according to Pew, "**Americans tend to believe that crime is up, even when official data shows it is down.** In 23 of 27 Gallup surveys conducted since 1993, at least 60% of U.S. adults have said there is more crime nationally than there was the year before, despite the downward trend in crime rates during most of that period" (emphasis added). [339]

Exception: Mass shootings have increased, with a toll on Americans' mental health

Despite the overall reductions in violent and property crimes in the U.S. over the last three decades, highly publicized incidents of mass shootings[340] fuel public fears and perceptions of a high crime rate. Notably:

- Thirteen of the deadliest mass shootings in the U.S. have occurred since 2015 and there were 42 mass shootings in 2023.[341]

- In 2021, the U.S. had over four gun deaths per 100,000, compared to 0.005 in Japan, 0.010 in South Korea, 0.013 in the UK, and 0.57 in Canada.[342]

- While the U.S. rate is high compared to other advanced democracies, there are 27 countries with higher rates of gun deaths, particularly in Central America, the Caribbean, Mexico, Venezuela, and the Philippines due to gangs and drug trafficking.[343]

- The U.S. has, by far, the highest number of civilian-held firearms in the world, with more guns than people—120 guns per 100 people. By comparison, Japan has 0.3 per 100, South Korea has 0.2, United Kingdom has 5.03, and Canada has 34.7.[344]

- A 2021 study found that the now expired "Federal Assault Weapons Ban that included a ban on large capacity magazines… from 1994 to 2004 resulted in a significant decrease in public mass shootings …. [M]ass shootings have a tremendous toll on American mental health." The study estimated that "a continuation of the federal ban could have prevented 30 public mass shootings."[345]

- A January 2024 study shows that 65% of registered voters support banning assault-style weapons, including 61% of independent voters, and a plurality of Republican voters.[346]

Trump and Harris Positions on Assault Weapons

One common sense measure already supported by a majority of independent voters and a majority of Americans is to renew the assault weapons ban that was in place from 1994 to 2004. **Assault weapons are weapons of war designed to kill as many people as possible, as quickly as possible; they are not weapons used for self-defense or hunting.**

- **Donald Trump** opposes an assault weapons ban,[347] or even raising the age to purchase an assault weapon to 21. In 2018, he mocked a Republican Senator for being too afraid of the National Rifle Association to raise the assault weapon purchase age to 21, but backpedaled a few days later[348] and in May 2024 gratefully accepted the NRA's endorsement—despite the NRA's plummeting membership and a 2024 jury verdict finding the NRA leadership liable for corruptly misspending millions in donated funds for their own personal use.[349]

- **Harris supports renewing the assault weapons ban.[350]**

§ 11: DEFENSE AND GLOBAL STABILITY: Alliances v. Isolationism

(Read Time: 20 minutes)

Peace Through a Strong Defense and Durable Alliances

Our nation recently celebrated the 80th anniversary of D-Day, when American soldiers joined with our allies to launch the liberation of Europe and destruction of the Nazi regime dedicated to global domination, genocide, and tyranny.

We learned as a nation during World War II that it is in America's national interest to defend freedom and democracy throughout the world. **America's isolationism** during the 1930s delayed our entry into the war until Japan attacked Pearl Harbor on December 7, 1941; by that time, continental Europe had fallen to Hitler and Britain was barely hanging on.

It was only with America's entrance into the war after Pearl Harbor that the Nazis and Imperial Japan were stopped, and democracy was saved. Had America's involvement been delayed any further, Germany may have perfected the atomic bomb first, and American democracy—and all the world's democracies—would likely have ended.

Instead, **America's *just-in-time* leadership** during WWII saved our nation and the world's democracies, established new and thriving democracies in Germany and Japan (and later in South Korea), surged Western economic growth creating enormous markets for American exports, and gave rise to **NATO** (the North Atlantic Treaty Organization)—a powerful defensive alliance that contained the Soviet Union's global ambitions for more than four decades.

NATO and The Cold War

The North Atlantic Treaty establishing NATO was signed in Washington D.C., in 1949. NATO's 12 founding members were the U.S., Belgium, Canada, Denmark, France, Iceland, Italy, Luxembourg, the Netherlands, Norway, Portugal, and the United Kingdom, followed later by Greece, Turkey, West Germany, and Spain.

With the fall of the Soviet Union in 1991 and the emergence of new democracies in Eastern Europe, NATO further expanded, adding the Czech Republic, Hungary, Poland, Bulgaria, Estonia, Latvia, Lithuania, Romania, Slovakia, Slovenia, Albania, Croatia, Montenegro, North Macedonia and—**following the Russian invasion of Ukraine two years ago—Finland and Sweden.**

NATO is a collective security agreement aimed at deterring aggression. Under Article 5 of the treaty, an attack on any member country is considered an attack against them all and member countries are required to assist the attacked party by taking "individually and in concert with the other Parties, such action as it deems necessary, including the use of armed force, to restore and maintain the security of the North Atlantic area."[351]

Article 5 was extremely effective at deterring aggression against member states during the Cold War with the Soviet Union, and continues to deter Russia (and now China) from aggression against NATO members including the U.S.[352]

Russia's brutal and unprovoked invasion of Ukraine

Since Russia's brutal and unprovoked invasion of Ukraine two years ago, ground fighting and air strikes have killed over 31,000 Ukrainian soldiers (as of February 2024)[353] and inflicted over 30,000 civilian casualties, while 3.7 million people are internally displaced and 6.5 million have fled the country.[354]

Although Ukraine is not yet a member of NATO, the alliance has been instrumental in delivering humanitarian and non-lethal aid to Ukraine following Russia's full-scale invasion of Ukraine in 2022. In addition, **NATO's Article 5 collective security guarantee has enabled allies to send weapons to Ukraine without diminishing their individual security.**[355]

Ukraine, today, is the front line of the world's democracies. If Russia overruns Ukraine, it will show weakness and invite Russia's dictator, Vladimir Putin, to continue his expansionist aims in Europe. He lamented the collapse of the Soviet Union as the demise of what he called "historical Russia."[356] The collapse of Ukraine would also embolden China's aims in Asia.[357]   Put simply, **unwavering U.S. and NATO support for Ukraine, is the best strategy we have for avoiding direct U.S. engagement with Russia.**

Yet, there are some today urging America to forget the stark lessons of World War II, abandon NATO and Ukraine, and retreat to the pre-WWII path of isolationism—at the very time when an axis of nuclear-armed dictators in Russia, China, Iran, and North Korea again threaten the world's democracies. Witness J.D. Vance's isolationist and naïve statement, "I don't really care what happens to Ukraine."[358]

Fortunately, about two-thirds of Americans continue to see the strategic importance of U.S. membership in NATO, recognizing that containing the autocratic and expansionist ambitions of Russia, China, Iran, and North Korea requires unity.[359]   In other words, Americans support peace through strong alliances.

China's Aggressive Behavior

In addition to Russia's ongoing threat to democracies in the North Atlantic Alliance, the U.S. faces a major strategic threat in the Pacific—China's aggressive behavior in the South China Sea, the East China Sea, and across the Taiwan Strait.[360] The United States has strong national and economic interests in defending the freedom of navigation and territorial integrity of our democratic allies and key trading partners in the Indo-Pacific region including Japan, the Philippines, Australia, and Taiwan.

Growing Threat from North Korea's nuclear weapons

The U.S. has strong national and economic interests in the stability of Japan and South Korea—our 4th and 6th largest trading partners—and is obligated by mutual defense treaties to defend both nations.[361] North Korea's threat to South Korea, Japan, and the western United States became significantly more serious in 2006 when it tested nuclear weapons and more recently, with the testing of an intercontinental ballistic missile system in 2022.[362]

North Korea's totalitarian, nuclear-armed leader, Kim Jong Un, "maintains fearful obedience by using threats of torture, executions, imprisonment, enforced disappearances, and forced labor. [He] systematically denies basic liberties, including freedom of expression, association, and religion."[363]

Trump's Dangerous Isolationism and Support of Autocrats

- **Trump Repudiates NATO which has kept the peace for 75 years:** At a February 2024 rally in South Carolina, Donald Trump said that when he was president, he told the leader of a large NATO country that if the country were "delinquent" in its payments to NATO and Russia attacked it, "I would not protect you. In fact, I would encourage them to do whatever the hell they want."[364]

- **Trump's statement** is **factually incorrect and strategically dangerous**. NATO members are not required to spend 2% of GDP on defense; 2% is a goal, not a treaty obligation; the treaty obligation is mutual defense. Moreover, Trump's statement was a **blatant repudiation of the Article 5 mutual defense obligation** that has deterred Russian aggression and avoided a third world war for the last 75 years.

- **Trump's Bizarre Failure on North Korea:** In 2018, Donald Trump met with North Korean dictator Kim Jong Un in Singapore, bizarrely declared they "fell in love," claimed he would achieve denuclearization, but walked away from this "summit" with nothing.[365]

- **Trump is drawn to autocrats and dictators:** Former Marine Corps General John Kelly, who was President Donald Trump's longest serving White House Chief of Staff, told CNN that Trump "has no idea what America stands for.... admires autocrats and murderous dictators.... has nothing but contempt for our democratic institutions, our Constitution, and the rule of law."[366]

Biden-Harris Administration has Strengthened Stable Alliances

- **The Biden-Harris Administration has boosted NATO** to its strongest position ever, negotiated NATO's expansion to include Finland and Sweden,[367] and has led the coalition in providing military and humanitarian support to Ukraine.

- **In the Indo-Pacific region,** in order to contain China's expansionism and maintain stability, the Biden-Harris Administration launched in 2024 a **new trilateral alliance** with Japan and the Philippines,[368] and in 2021 announced **AUKUS,** a new security partnership with the U.K. and Australia, leading to a new fleet of conventionally armed, nuclear-powered submarines.[369]

- In 2023, **Joe Biden** and **South Korean President Yoon Suk Yeol** reaffirmed the two nations' mutual defense treaty and strengthened economic ties through the Indo-Pacific Economic Framework.[370]

§ 12: MILITARY SERVICEMEMBERS & VETERANS

(Read Time: 6 minutes)

"To care for him who shall have borne the battle and for his widow and his orphan." - Abraham Lincoln, 2d inaugural address

Over the course of American history, more than one million Americans have given their lives[371] to preserve and protect the fundamental rights we too often take for granted: equal protection under the laws; the right to elect our leaders; the freedoms of speech, press, and assembly; free exercise of religion without government interference; and equal opportunity to become part of the American middle class.

Americans in uniform gave us independence from Great Britain in the 18th century; saved the Union and abolished slavery in the 19th century; defeated the Nazis and Imperial Japan in the 20th century; and, since World War II, have worked to maintain global stability by containing threats from communist autocrats, dictators, and terrorists.

America has a history of caring for servicemembers wounded in the service of our nation. The Continental Congress in 1776 encouraged enlistments during the Revolutionary War by providing pensions for disabled veterans.[372] In 1865, President Abraham Lincoln authorized the first medical facility to provide care to discharged members of the Army and Navy and, in his second inaugural address called on Americans "to care for him who shall have borne the battle and for his widow and his orphan"—the words displayed at the main entrance of the Department of Veterans Affairs.[373]

Caring for veterans and honoring the service of our fallen soldiers has always been an American value and a **norm for candidates of** *all* **political parties—until now.** The records of the candidates are revealing.

Donald Trump on military service and caring for veterans

- Donald Trump has mocked American soldiers who gave their lives and limbs in the service of our country as "losers" and suckers." This has been verified numerous times from multiple sources; the attitude is so repulsive, it is no wonder Trump is running away from his own words:

  - During the World War I centennial in 2018, Donald Trump canceled a trip to the American Cemetery near Paris, telling senior staff members, "Why should I go to that cemetery? It's filled with losers." In a separate conversation on the same trip, Donald Trump referred to the 1,800 marines who lost their lives as "suckers" for getting killed.[374]

  - In 2015, Donald Trump expressed contempt for the war record of the late Senator John McCain and GOP presidential nominee, who spent more than five years as a prisoner of war in Vietnam and declined an offer to be set free before his fellow prisoners.[375] "He's not a war hero," Donald Trump said while running for the Republican nomination for president. "I like people who weren't captured."[376]

  - U.S. Marine Corps General John Kelly, who was the longest serving White House Chief of Staff for President Donald Trump (2017-19), and who lost his own son, First Lieutenant Robert Kelly, to a land mine in Afghanistan, confirmed Donald Trump's disparaging remarks about fallen soldiers and disabled veterans in a 2023 interview with

CNN. He told CNN that Donald Trump believes "those who defend their country in uniform, or are shot down or seriously wounded in combat, or spend years being tortured as POWs are all 'suckers' because 'there is nothing in it for them.'"[377]

○ In 2023, retiring Chairman of the Joint Chiefs of Staff Mark Milley, in an interview with *The Atlantic*, recounted Donald Trump's disparaging remarks about a disabled veteran who had lost a leg in an attack in Afghanistan. According to General Milley, Donald Trump asked, "Why do you bring people like that here? No one wants to see that, the wounded."[378]

The Biden-Harris Administration on military service and caring for veterans

• In 2022, the Biden-Harris Administration signed the **bipartisan PACT Act**, the most significant expansion of benefits and services for veterans in more than 30 years.[379] The new law provides medical care and disability benefits for medical conditions resulting from environmental exposures to burn pits near military bases—including various respiratory related conditions, and several forms of cancer, including reproductive cancers, melanoma, pancreatic cancer, kidney cancer, and brain cancers such as glioblastoma.

§ 13: CLIMATE: Escalating Floods, Wildfires, Droughts, & Violent Weather

(Read Time: 9 minutes)

There is a fundamental distinction between weather and climate: *"Weather"* refers to daily and weekly temperature and precipitation changes; *"climate"* refers to **long-term averages** over years, decades, centuries, and millennia.

The "climate change" phenomenon refers to the steady increase in average global temperatures since the beginning of the Industrial Revolution in the mid-1700s. A cold snap of a few days or weeks is irrelevant to **long-term global-warming trends** that are leading to increased drought, wildfires, crop failures, intense storms, rising sea levels, floods, coastal erosion, and landslides.

What Is Global Warming?

- **Fossil fuels**—coal, oil, and natural gas (mostly methane)— are burned to create heat, light, power engines, and generate electricity.

- Burning fossil fuels **releases carbon dioxide (CO2)** into the earth's atmosphere—which began with the start of the industrial revolution in the mid-1700s.

- Carbon dioxide has a **"greenhouse effect"** that **traps warm air**, not allowing heat generated by sunlight to escape the earth's atmosphere.

- That is why coal, oil, and natural gas (methane) are referred to as **"greenhouse gases."**

- **Methane,** released by cattle raising and during natural gas production, is a **powerful greenhouse gas**, responsible for about **30%** of the rise in global temperatures since the beginning of the industrial revolution.[380]

- In 2019, atmospheric **CO2 concentrations** were higher than at any time **in at least two million years,** and concentrations of methane were higher than at any time in the last **800,000 years**.[381]

The Evidence

The Intergovernmental Panel on Climate Change[382]—the world's most authoritative scientific body on climate change—issued the following findings on global warming in 2023:

- It is "unequivocal" that human influence, largely from the burning of fossil fuels, is warming the atmosphere, ocean, and land.

- The last decade has been warmer than any period for about 125,000 years.

- Oceans are warming faster than at any time since the end of the last ice age (12,000 years ago).

- Sea levels have been rising faster than any prior century for 3,000 years.[383]

Floods, wildfires, and violent weather are increasing in the United States

The oceans are locked in a vicious cycle where warming temperatures are melting arctic ice, the dark ocean water underneath the ice absorbs more heat, and the warming ocean water leads to still more ice melting. Arctic summer ice could disappear as soon as 2035.[384] **The warming of the oceans is leading to extreme weather in North America—as well as Europe and Asia.**[385]

Last year, scientists at the National Oceanic and Atmospheric Administration released the following findings:[386]

- *The impacts of weather extremes...are far-reaching across every region of the United States.*

- ***Rising Sea Levels Are Already "Besieging the American South":*** *One of the most rapid sea level surges on Earth is besieging the American South, forcing a reckoning for coastal communities across eight U.S. states... [F]rom Texas to North Carolina, sea levels are at least 6 inches higher than they were in 2010" leading to choked septic systems, insurance companies raising rates or withdrawing coverage, flooded roads, and marooned drivers.*[387] *The rising water level is mostly due to a combination of melt water from glaciers and ice sheets, and expansion of seawater as it warms.*[388] *(In addition, due to water run-off patterns, water levels on the Great Lakes are also expected to rise.*[389]*)*

- ***Hurricanes*** *have been intensifying more rapidly since the 1980s and causing heavier rainfall and higher storm surges.*[390]

- ***Extreme floods*** *are happening more often than current climate models would suggest, with grave implications for everything from roads and bridges to failing dams to the rising cost of flood insurance.*[391]

- *Cost to the Economy: "The impacts of extreme climate events are costing the nation an estimated $150 billion each year (and) with every increment of global warming, costly damages are expected to accelerate."* [392] Last year (2023) was a historic year of U.S. billion-dollar weather and climate disasters.[393]

June 2023 through May 2024 has been the hottest 12 months on record: "Data released by European climate scientists showed May (2024) was the 12th consecutive month during which average global temperatures surpassed all observations since 1850, and probably **any extended period for more than 100,000 years**" (emphasis added).[394]

The solutions needed to mitigate the effects of global warming are clear and most of the needed technologies are already available:[395]

1. Retire coal plants or add carbon-capture technology to existing plants.[396]

2. Invest in zero-emission renewable energy (solar, wind, hydroelectric, geothermal, tidal).[397]

3. Invest in next-generation nuclear energy.[398]

4. Invest in energy-efficient heating and cooling upgrades for buildings,[399] including "cool roofs."[400]

5. Invest in advanced transmission to reduce electricity waste.[401]

6. Invest in technologies to reduce CO_2 emissions in materials production (cement, steel & plastics).[402]

7. Shift gasoline-powered cars to electric vehicles (powered by an electric grid using clean energy).[403]

8. Shift heavy transportation (planes, ships, trucks, and trains) to hydrogen fuel (made from H20).[404]

9. Shift buses to electricity (from a clean electric grid) or hydrogen (made from H2O).[405]

10. Halt destruction of rain forests especially in the Amazon (which absorb a tremendous amount of CO_2)[406] and require that each mature tree cut down be replaced by multiple new trees.

11. Reduce food waste (rotting food in landfills emits methane).[407]

12. Eat more plant-based foods and invest in new feed technologies to reduce methane emissions from cattle.[408]

Trump Actions to Exacerbate U.S. Flooding, Wildfires, and Violent Weather

- **Donald Trump,** based on his numerous statements over many years,[409] confuses short-term weather variations with long-term climate changes and **denies the facts about global warming.**

- As President, he **pulled the U.S. out of international efforts** to curb global warming.[410]

- Trump **loosened the controls on methane leakage** (the most potent greenhouse gas)—eventually reversed by Congress in 2021.[411]

- Trump **rolled back fuel efficiency requirements** for vehicle emissions, the largest source of greenhouse gases in the U.S.—later reversed by the Biden-Harris Administration.[412]

- In addition, in 2024, he indicated he would take actions to **make the effects of climate change worse**, promising oil company executives he was soliciting for billion-dollar campaign contributions that he would repeal environmental regulations to curb global warming and pollution.[413]

Biden-Harris Actions to Address Increased Flooding, Wildfires, and Violent Weather

- **The Biden-Harris Administration** signed into law the Inflation Reduction Act of 2022, **the largest ever investment in clean energy and greenhouse gas reduction**—$370 billion aimed at reducing greenhouse gas emissions, paid for by closing tax loopholes and imposing a minimum tax on corporations that had been paying no tax.[414] The law:

  - Creates tax incentives for private industry to produce **more renewable energy**.

  - Rewards oil and gas companies for **reducing methane** emissions.

  - Provides **subsidies to farmers** to reduce emissions.

  - Gives **tax incentives to consumers** to use more renewable energy by purchasing electric vehicles, and installing solar panels and heat pumps.[415]

§ 14: INFRASTRUCTURE, COMPETITIVENESS, & ENERGY INDEPENDENCE

(Read Time: 9 minutes)

Gallup reports that 69% of Americans identify the "availability and affordability of energy" as an issue they worry about a "great deal" or a "fair amount."[416] The larger issue is ensuring America has the infrastructure and energy independence to succeed in a highly competitive global marketplace.

Infrastructure

Every four years, the American Society of Civil Engineers—a nonpartisan organization of engineers—publishes a report card on the state of America's infrastructure. In its most recent report, March of 2021, the engineers gave the following grades:

- "A" (fit for the future)—no U.S. sectors received a grade of A.

- "B" (good, adequate for now)—**ports** and **rail**.

- "C" (mediocre)—**bridges, drinking water, energy, solid waste disposal**; and

- "D" (poor and at risk)—**airports, dams, hazardous waste disposal, inland waterways, levees, public parks, roads, schools, stormwater management, transit,** and **wastewater management**.[417]

A major national investment to improve America's infrastructure did not occur until November of the Biden-Harris Administration's first year in office when a **$1.2 trillion bipartisan infrastructure deal was signed into law.**[418]

Trump's Broken Promise: Inaction on Infrastructure

- **Donald Trump promised** to be the "builder President." "We are going to fix our inner cities and rebuild our highways, bridges, tunnels, airports, schools, hospitals," he said in his 2016 election night victory speech. "And we will put millions of our people to work as we rebuild it."[419] While promising investments of $1 to $1.5 trillion, he never proposed more than $20 billion per year in federal funding and **failed to enact** even that. One urban planner said, "This (Donald Trump) Administration has been **a major letdown for nearly all state and local officials and advocates**" (emphasis added).[420]

Biden-Harris Landmark Bipartisan Infrastructure Law

- In November 2021, President Joe Biden signed into law the Infrastructure Investment and Jobs Act (*also known as* the Bipartisan Infrastructure Law), making $1.2 trillion in infrastructure investments, the **largest national investment in infrastructure in U.S. history.** The new bipartisan law includes the following investments: [421]

  ○ $110 billion in **roads and bridges,** including congestion relief in cities;

  ○ $66 billion in **passenger and freight rail**;

  ○ $65 billion to make the **nation's electric grid** more reliable and resilient;

- ○ $65 billion to expand broadband internet to **rural and low-income communities;**

- ○ $55 billion for **clean drinking water,** including lead-pipe replacement;

- ○ $47 billion to **protect infrastructure from cyberattacks, floods and fires;**

- ○ $39 billion for **public transit;**

- ○ $29 billion for **airport improvements;**

- ○ $21 billion to clean up **hazardous waste** sites, mines, and old oil and gas wells;

- ○ $17 billion to improve **ports;**

- ○ $8 billion to **mitigate droughts** in the West;

- ○ $7.5 billion for **electric vehicle charging** stations;

- ○ $5 billion for **electric school buses;** and

- ○ $3 billion for **dams.**[422]

U.S. Dependence on Foreign Computer Chips ("semiconductors")

Most of today's electronic devices—computers, smart phones, cars, planes, LED lights, and solar cells—rely on "semiconductors." Because of their common use in computers, semiconductors are often called "computer chips."

About 37% of the world's semiconductors were manufactured in the United States in 1990 versus only 12% in 2020. The U.S. is now heavily reliant on Asia.

In 2020, the last year of Donald Trump's term, there were acute global shortages of semiconductors, caused by soaring demand and a lack of investors willing to build the multibillion-dollar factories needed to make the components.[423]

Biden-Harris Invested in Domestic Chip Industry After Trump Reduced Supplies and Increased Prices

- **The Biden-Harris Administration,** in August of 2022, signed into law the **bipartisan "Chips and Science Act"** providing $52 billion in subsidies to spur construction of more than a half-dozen semiconductor manufacturing facilities in the United States and provide **more secure domestic supplies of computer chips**. The bill also authorized tens of billions of dollars to support federal research and development in next-generation quantum computing and artificial intelligence.

- **Donald Trump,** as part of his 2018 trade war with China, imposed 25% tariffs on semiconductor imports—**reducing supplies and pushing up prices**.[424]

- In short, Donald Trump's actions exacerbated the shortage of computer chips in the U.S. and raised prices; the Biden-Harris Administration brought Democrats and Republicans together to make a massive national investment in rebuilding the domestic semiconductor industry.

Energy Independence and Gas Prices

Many believe, *incorrectly*, that the U.S. achieved "energy independence" under Donald Trump and lost it under Biden-Harris. As explained below, the trend towards U.S. energy independence—producing more energy than we consume—began long before the Trump Administration and energy independence has increased under the Biden-Harris Administration.

- "While it is technically correct to say the U.S. became energy independent while Trump was in office, **the reason was the shale boom that had begun in earnest in 2005**.... In 2019, the U.S. produced more energy than we consumed for the first time since at least the 1940s. It had been a steady march since 2005, when net U.S. energy imports hit a record high. But the shale boom unleashed vast amounts of domestic oil and gas, and by 2012 U.S. net imports had fallen to half the 2005 level... By the time President Trump took office in 2017, U.S. net energy imports had fallen 75% from the 2005 level... In 2022 [the second year of Biden-Harris], U.S. **net energy exports grew to...the highest number on record. Total U.S. energy production was also the highest on record**" (emphasis added). [425]

- **The public's misunderstanding about energy independence under Trump and Biden-Harris is due to gas prices spiking in 2022 following the Russian invasion of Ukraine.** A June 2022 analysis explained that "since the beginning of the Ukraine war, Russia has been selling less oil in part because of sanctions imposed by the European Union, United States, and other major economies. That has reduced global supplies and led to a jump in prices... [In addition] many [oil] executives believe that another [oil price crash] is inevitable. That has made them hesitant to drill new wells and seriously ramp up production....They also have th[e] expectation that electric vehicles are going to continue to grow, which means

that 10 years from now, that oil well may not be earning profits…. [A]ll of that is creating a disincentive to drill."[426]

- Bottom line: The post-pandemic surge in demand for gasoline, together with the reduced supply due to the Ukraine war,
  and a fall-off in investment by oil companies, have pushed
  up gasoline prices at the pump – even though **U.S. energy
  independence continues to grow.**

§ 15: POVERTY, HUNGER, HOMELESSNESS & DISABILITY PROGRAMS

(Read Time: 6 minutes)

> *"It was once said that the moral test of government is how that government treats those who are in the dawn of life, the children; those who are in the twilight of life, the elderly; and those who are in the shadows of life, the sick, the needy and the handicapped."* [427] -- Hubert H. Humphrey

Gallup reports that 80% of Americans worry a "great deal" or "a fair amount" about "hunger and homelessness." These concerns are especially acute for Americans with disabilities.

Following are key programs assisting low-income and disabled Americans with income support, nutrition, housing, and healthcare.

1. **Medicaid** is the major health and long-term care program for *low-income* children, families, seniors, and people with disabilities. It is financed jointly by the federal and state governments and administered by the states.[428]

2. **The Earned Income Tax Credit (EITC)** is a tax credit that reduces or eliminates taxes, or provides payments, to low-income working Americans to incentivize work.[429]

3. **The Supplemental Nutrition Assistance Program** ("SNAP," formerly Food Stamps) provides benefits to help

people in low-income households purchase food;[430] the national school lunch, school breakfast and summer food service programs provide nutrition to low-income children;[431] and the WIC program provides nutrition assistance for low-income women, infants, and children.[432]

4. **Housing Assistance** for low-income Americans includes public housing,[433] "Section 8" rent subsidies,[434] and homeless assistance grants to provide housing and services for homeless persons.

5. **Supplemental Security Income (SSI):** provides small monthly benefit payments to low-income individuals who are aged, blind, or disabled.[435]

6. **Temporary Assistance for Needy Families** (TANF) program, a part of 1990s "welfare reform," replaced the old cash benefit program (AFDC) with a block grant to states for benefits that are temporary, while seeking employment.[436]

7. **The Individuals with Disabilities Education Act** (IDEA) authorizes federal grants to support the education of children with disabilities. As a condition of receiving funds, states must agree to provide students with Individual Education Plans to ensure a free appropriate public education. (Unfortunately, while the statute committed the federal government to pay 40 percent of the average per pupil expenditure for special education, that pledge has never been fulfilled—with current funding at 13 percent.)[437]

8. **Social Security Disability Insurance** provides monthly income support to former workers (and adult children of retired workers) with disabilities that prevent or limit their ability to work.[438]

9. **Low-Income Home Energy Assistance (LIHEAP)** is aimed at assisting very low-income households that pay a high proportion of household income for energy.[439]

Trump actions impacting low-income and disabled Americans

- The Trump Administration put in a place a rule that would have **cut food stamps (SNAP) for 700,000 people**. The rule was eventually blocked by the courts and reversed by the Biden-Harris Administration.[440]

- Overtime pay is important for keeping low- and moderate-income workers out of poverty. As President, Trump issued a new **rule leaving eight million workers ineligible for overtime pay** (reversed in 2024 by the Biden-Harris Administration).[441]

- Trump's failed attempt to repeal the Affordable Care Act in 2017 would have imposed major **cuts in Medicaid health coverage** impacting millions of low-income and disabled Americans.[442]

- At a campaign rally in South Carolina on November 24, 2015, Donald Trump openly **mocked the physical disabilities** of *New York Times* reporter Serge Kovaleski (click on the end note to link to the video record).[443]

- Donald Trump ignores the many reasons that individuals may lack equal opportunity—educational, medical, or economic disadvantages—and **simply calls poor people "morons."** [444]

Biden-Harris actions assisting low-income and disabled Americans

- In 2021, the Biden-Harris Administration signed the **American Rescue Plan Act (ARPA)** to speed up the country's recovery from the severe economic and health effects of the COVID-19 pandemic, which led to the **lowest child poverty rate** in American history through expansion of the Child Tax Credit.[445] Kamala Harris has proposed extending and expanding the Child Tax Credit. [446]

- The ARPA also **expanded the Affordable Care Act** leading to record-breaking health care enrollment, added funds for **Medicaid** to cover an additional one million uninsured Americans, and created the first-ever **summer nutrition benefit for students.**[447]

- Harris would restore the 2021 American Rescue Plan's **enhancement of the earned income tax credit (EITC)** which increased the maximum credit for workers without dependent children to roughly $1,500.[448]

- Harris has proposed **increasing the federal minimum wage**. According to a nonpartisan Congressional Budget Office study, a $15 minimum wage could lift Americans out of poverty.[449]

- Emergency Rental Assistance and other ARPA assistance helped over eight million renters stay in their homes during the pandemic. It has been called the **"deepest investment the federal government has made in low-income renters** since the nation launched its public housing system" (emphasis added).[450]

- The Biden-Harris Administration has taken numerous actions to improve opportunities for Americans with disabilities including:[451]

  - Increased annual funding for Individuals with Disabilities Education Act (IDEA) grants by $1.4 billion.

  - Helping schools to access Medicaid funding to increase access to mental health and disability services in schools.

  - New protections for airline passengers with disabilities[452] and accessibility improvements at 111 rail stations.

§ 16: GOOD GOVERNMENT Requires Bipartisanship, Upholding the Rule of Law, and Effective, Ethical Leadership

(Read Time: 12 minutes)

Gallup found that having good government leadership is one of Americans' top three concerns, together with the economy and immigration.[453]

Good government depends on three things:

1. **A President with the ability to build bipartisan consensus** among Democrats, Republicans, and Independents—without which there is little progress in solving problems.

2. **A President who respects the Constitution and the rule of law**—the foundations on which our nation is built, and on which our future depends.

3. **A President who appoints people with experience and high ethical standards to run the federal agencies** that defend our nation; care for our veterans; respond to disasters; issue benefit checks; provide health coverage; inspect food, drugs, and drinking water; and work cooperatively with states to build roads, airports, and water systems, and educate our children.

Records on Bipartisanship

Trump Presided Over Longest Federal Shutdown and Blocked Bipartisan Immigration Reform

- As President, Donald Trump presided over the longest shutdown of the Federal government—34 days—**unable to negotiate federal spending bills** with Congress.

- Trump's signature legislation as President was a highly **partisan** tax cut bill[454] that increased the public debt by nearly $1.9 trillion.[455]

- In 2024, former President Trump urged GOP Senators to **kill the most significant *bipartisan* immigration agreement in years**, which would have provided desperately needed resources to tighten the southern border and resolve an enormous backlog of immigration cases; he prevented this progress to preserve the issue for his campaign.[456]

Biden-Harris Record: 5 Major Bipartisan Successes in 3 Years

- In **2021,** the Biden-Harris Administration signed into law the Infrastructure Investment and Jobs Act (also known as the **Bipartisan Infrastructure Law**), making $1.2 trillion in infrastructure investments, the **largest national investment in infrastructure in U.S. history.**

- In **2022,** the Biden-Harris Administration signed into law the **bipartisan Chips and Science Act,** providing $52 billion in subsidies to spur construction of more than a half-dozen semiconductor manufacturing facilities in the United States, providing a more secure domestic supply of computer chips which are essential to all modern electronics.

- In **2022**, the Biden-Harris Administration signed the bipartisan PACT Act, the most **significant expansion of benefits and services for veterans** in more than 30 years (see §11 for details).[457]

- In **2023**, the Biden-Harris Administration negotiated the **bipartisan Fiscal Responsibility Act** with House Republicans which avoided a dangerous Treasury default and has slowed federal discretionary spending growth.[458]

- In **2024**, the Biden-Harris Administration signed a bipartisan Federal Aviation Administration reauthorization for **airport modernization**, technology programs, and safety.[459]

Respect for the Constitution and the Rule of Law

Donald Trump:

- **Unanimously found guilty by a jury of 34 felony counts** of falsifying business records (May 30, 2024).[460]

- **Ordered to pay $355 million** for a years-long scheme **fraudulently reporting** the value of his properties (February 16, 2024).[461]

- **Called for termination of the Constitution** of the United States in order to overturn the results of the 2020 election (December 3, 2022).[462]

- **Twice impeached by House of Representatives** for "**Abuse of Power** and Obstruction of Congress," and "**Incitement of Insurrection**" (December 18, 2019, and January 13, 2021).[463] In the Senate, his followers protected him from removal, with a two-thirds vote being required.

- **Indicted by Georgia grand jury** for election subversion in Fulton County, Georgia (August 14, 2023).[464]

- **Indicted by federal grand jury for taking, and refusing return of, classified documents** (June 9, 2023).[465]

- **Illegally withheld funds** appropriated for Ukraine's defense, as determined by the Comptroller General of the United States (Jan. 16, 2020).[466]

- **Plotted to overturn the 2020 election**, as concluded by the bipartisan House Select Committee to Investigate the January 6th Attack on the United States Capitol. Excerpts from the bipartisan report follow.[467]

  ○ *Beginning election night and continuing through January 6th and thereafter, Donald Trump purposely disseminated false allegations of fraud related to the 2020 Presidential election in order to aid his effort to overturn the election and for purposes of soliciting contributions. These false claims provoked his supporters to violence on January 6th.*

  ○ *Knowing that he and his supporters had lost dozens of election lawsuits, and despite his own senior advisors refuting his election fraud claims and urging him to concede his election loss, Donald Trump refused to accept the lawful result of the 2020 election. Rather than honor his constitutional obligation to "take Care that the Laws be faithfully executed," President Donald Trump instead plotted to overturn the election outcome.*

  ○ *Despite knowing that such an action would be illegal, and that no State had or would submit an altered electoral slate, Donald Trump corruptly pressured Vice President Mike Pence to refuse to count electoral votes during Congress's joint session on January 6th.*

  ○ *Donald Trump unlawfully pressured State officials and legislators to change the results of the election in their States.*

- ○ *Donald Trump oversaw an effort to obtain and transmit false electoral certificates to Congress and the National Archives.*

- ○ *Knowing that violence was underway at the Capitol, and despite his duty to ensure that the laws are faithfully executed, Donald Trump refused repeated requests over a multiple hour period that he instruct his violent supporters to disperse and leave the Capitol, and instead watched the violent attack unfold on television. This failure to act perpetuated the violence at the Capitol and obstructed Congress's proceeding to count electoral votes.*

- ○ *President Donald Trump had authority and responsibility to direct deployment of the National Guard in the District of Columbia, but never gave any order to deploy the National Guard on January 6th.*

- After Congress reconvened on January 6, 2021, **the worst assault in U.S. history on the constitutional right to vote and the rule of law occurred** when 7 Senators and 139 Representatives, all Trump supporters, sought to overturn the will of the people, voting against certification of the 2020 presidential election results, based on spurious claims of election fraud—claims that had failed in dozens of court challenges and four re-counts.[468]

Appointing People with Experience and High Ethical Standards

Donald Trump:

- As summarized by *Bloomberg News* in 2019, "Donald Trump promised to drain the Washington swamp. Instead, he has surrounded himself with family members, appointees and advisers who've been accused of conflicts of interest, misuse of public funds, influence peddling, self-enrichment, working for foreign governments, failure to disclose information, and violating ethics rules." Accusations of corruption were leveled at EPA Administrator Scott Pruitt, Commerce Secretary Wilbur Ross, Interior Secretary Ryan Zinke, HHS Secretary Tom Price, National Security Advisor Michael Flynn, CFPB Director Mick Mulvaney, HUD Secretary Ben Carson, Education Secretary Betsy DeVos, Treasury Secretary Steve Mnuchin, FEMA Administrator Brock Long, and Special Adviser Carl Icahn. Follow this link for details: https://www.bloomberg. com/graphics/Donald Trump-administration-conflicts/.[469]

Biden-Harris Administration:

- The Biden-Harris Administration began with an executive order on ethics, committing their administration to high standards in doing the public's business and avoiding personal conflicts of interest.[470]

CONCLUSION

(Read Time: 5 minutes)

As I noted at the beginning of this book, I am an independent voter and have supported presidential candidates of both political parties. In my professional life I have worked for Administrations and U.S. Senators of both political parties and have enjoyed collaborating with people of goodwill in both parties who are dedicated to solving problems and moving the country forward.

This year's presidential election is unique and pivotal. **In my four decades working with national leaders on both sides of the aisle, I have never seen such a stark contrast between the two major party candidates for president.** Based on the factual records of the Trump and Biden-Harris Administrations, and the statements of Trump and Harris as candidates for President, the choice before us could not be clearer:

 A Trump-Vance victory would resume policies of the first Trump term, leading to:

- **Rising consumer prices (inflation)** caused by huge new tariffs on imported goods and labor shortages caused by mass expulsions of workers.

- **Forcing on all Americans a particular religious viewpoint on abortion** leading to a loss of freedom in family planning and reproductive healthcare decisions.

- **Risk of a new world war**, with the foolish **isolationism** of Donald Trump and J.D. Vance increasing the risk of Ukraine falling, Moscow attempting to re-occupy parts of Eastern Europe, and China invading Taiwan.

- **Forcible expulsion from America of 11 million** women, children, and men—triggering inflation, business closures, recession, and a humanitarian disaster.

- **Exploding the public debt** (which already increased 50% in Donald Trump's first term) due to unnecessary tax cuts for corporations and the wealthiest Americans.

- **Earlier bankruptcy** of the Social Security and Medicare Trust Funds by depleting payroll trust fund revenues.

- **Deep cuts in federal funding for local schools** (including rural and charter schools and special education for disabled students).

- **Escalating climate emergencies**—wildfires consuming the West, chronic flooding in the South, dangerous heat and violent weather across the U.S.—caused by cutting funding for clean energy technologies and U.S. withdrawal from global climate agreements.

- **Decaying U.S. roads, bridges, airports, and water systems** due to rolling back, or failing to implement, bipartisan investments in infrastructure.

- **Placing our government**—which we depend on for national defense, benefit payments, student loans, law enforcement, roads and water systems, and food and drug safety—in the hands of Trump cronies, under the direction of Donald Trump, who, as a reminder, was convicted by a unanimous jury on 34 counts of falsifying business records.

- **The risk of America's democracy ending.** The bipartisan House January 6th Committee concluded, "Trump corruptly pressured Vice President Mike Pence to refuse to count electoral votes during Congress's joint session on January 6th."[471]

J.D. Vance's statements imply, unlike Pence, that he would have yielded to Trump's pressure and refused to follow the will of the voters.[472]

A Harris-Walz victory would continue policies of the Biden-Harris Administration, with some additions to provide further relief to low- and middle-income Americans:

- **Providing strong, steady leadership** of NATO—protecting Ukraine and Europe's democracies—and strengthening America's Pacific alliances, in order to avoid a catastrophic war with Russia or China.

- **Keeping inflation and unemployment low**, and the economy growing steadily.

- **Avoiding explosive increases in the public debt**, by not extending unnecessary tax cuts for the wealthiest Americans.

- **Continuing the steady reduction in unlawful border crossings**—now at the lowest levels since 2020, with Harris signing the bipartisan border security bill.[473]

- **Expanding access to reproductive healthcare**, without interference from state politicians.

- **Restoring the U.S. computer chip industry** which had become deeply dependent on foreign imports prior to the Biden-Harris Administration's bipartisan investments.

- **Rebuilding decaying roads, bridges, airports, and water systems and boosting U.S. competitiveness** by implementing the bipartisan infrastructure agreement.

- **Slowing climate-induced floods, fires, and increasingly violent weather** across the United States by implementing historic investments in clean technologies.

- **Enacting measures to improve the affordability of housing** for renters and first-time buyers.

- **Healing divisions** by treating **all people** with **respect** and reaching across party lines to enact **bipartisan agreements**.

One final, but especially important point: If you choose not to vote, or vote for a 3rd party candidate or a write-in, as a practical matter, your decision may advance the major party candidate you do *not* want to win. Ask yourself if you want to impact the outcome of this election, or not? As an independent voter, I intend to impact the outcome; how about you?

ABOUT THE AUTHOR:
From One Independent
Voter to Another

(Read Time: 5 minutes)

My own political journey began in 1983, when I moved from Ohio to Washington, D.C., after law school to work in the U.S. Senate.

The 1980s, and into the early 1990s, was a very different time, when Democrats and Republicans—especially in the Senate—routinely worked together and both political parties were diverse. There were conservatives, moderates, and liberals in the Republican Party, and likewise a diversity of political views in the Democratic Party; and Senate chairmanships were largely filled by "work horses" rather than "show horses."

I started out as one of two attorneys on the Republican staff of the Senate Budget Committee for Chairman Pete V. Domenici (R-NM), at a time when the House and Senate Budget Committees were active and vital committees, developing congressional budget plans to set annual parameters for spending, revenues, and debt, and engineering multi-committee deficit reduction packages. Chairman Domenici was an unapologetic fiscal hawk but was known as a straight shooter who routinely met with his Democratic counterpart at the House Budget Committee to hammer out bipartisan budget plans.

When Republicans lost the Senate majority in the 1986 election, my job was lost with the majority because the staff was cut in half, and I was a recent hire. I moved over to the minority staff[474] of the Senate Rules and Administration Committee, where longtime Alaska

Senator Ted Stevens had just become the Ranking Republican. Stevens had a reputation for being mercurial on the Senate Floor but was a fine boss and a highly effective Senator, and was the ultimate work horse—collaborating closely with his Democratic counterparts to move legislation.

(In fact, Republican Stevens and Democratic Senator Danny Inouye of Hawaii worked together so well, as Chair and Ranking Member of the Defense Appropriations Subcommittee, that Stevens traveled to Hawaii to campaign for Inouye's reelection. The explanation for this extraordinary bipartisanship: they were both part of the "greatest generation" that served in World War II and put country ahead of party.)

Stevens was also an ardent advocate for the State of Alaska which has unique needs due to its size, strategic location (adjacent to Russia), diverse Native population, challenging climate, and small economy. I remained on Stevens' committee staff for six years, becoming his Chief Counsel at the Rules Committee, where I assisted him with Senate institutional issues and advised him on federal budget, tax, and trade legislation.

In 1993, I took the unusual step of jumping over the partisan aisle and went to work as General Counsel and federal budget advisor for Democratic Senator Daniel Patrick Moynihan when he assumed the Chairmanship of the Senate Finance Committee, which oversees federal legislation relating to the tax code, Social Security, Medicare, Medicaid, income support programs, and international trade. Moynihan, who had previously served in both Democratic and Republican Administrations (Kennedy, Johnson, Nixon, and Ford), had no concern about my previous service on Republican committee staffs and, like me, had a strong inclination towards bipartisan collaboration.

In 1995, after two years with Chairman Moynihan, I moved downtown to the Clinton White House to serve on the legislative affairs staff of the Office of Management and Budget, where I remained for more than four years as Assistant OMB Director, advocating for the President's budget priorities, and shepherding the President's legislative policy statements through the internal White House clearance process.

In 1999, Senator Moynihan asked me to return to the Senate Finance Committee where he was the Ranking Democrat (Democrats were then in the minority) to resume my duties as General Counsel and budget advisor, and also to serve as Chief Health Counsel. While I deeply enjoyed my time at the White House, working for Senator Moynihan again was something I couldn't pass up and I stayed in that position until his retirement in early 2001.

In late 2001, I jumped across the political aisle one more time, going to work in the Bush-43 Administration as Director of Congressional Affairs at the Corporation for National and Community Service, the parent agency for AmeriCorps, VISTA, and Senior Service Corps. While I had been quite comfortable with President Clinton's brand of Democratic centrism, going to work for President Bush at AmeriCorps was an easy decision, because Bush was (and remains) a strong proponent of volunteerism and civic engagement.

By now, you may be wondering if this sort of political ping pong is common in Washington. It is not. In fact, it is extremely uncommon. Party loyalty is deeply embedded in Washington and people's careers generally advance only through strong and continuing ties with one party or the other.

My decisions to work for Senators and Presidents on both sides of the aisle were due to my independent streak. I am moderate by nature—interested in hearing all points of view and perspectives, and far more interested in problem solving and consensus building than advancing a particular ideology or a particular political party.

While I affiliated with one party or the other earlier in my career, I now consider myself to be politically independent. From my perspective, both parties have become too ideologically entrenched— Republicans with isolationism, anti-immigrant hysteria, mixing religion and politics (which never works out well), and rejection of climate science; and Democrats on the extreme left too focused on identity politics.

Fortunately, while politicians and media emphasize partisan division, Americans are *not* hopelessly divided. As laid out in §1 of this book, solid majorities of Americans continue to share the fundamental values that have sustained our republic for nearly 250 years: the right to equal protection under the laws, the right to vote for a representative government, the freedoms of speech, press and assembly, the right to free exercise of religion without government interference, the right to privacy without government intrusion, and the opportunity to work hard and earn a place in America's middle class.

ENDNOTES: Links to Nonpartisan Sources

For readers who purchased *Independent Voters* as a Kindle eBook on Amazon, you can immediately access the internet links for the book's source material simply by clicking on the relevant endnote.

If you purchased *Independent Voters* as a print book on Amazon, you can quickly access the internet links in the book's endnotes at our website, IndependentVotersBook.com.

Note on sources frequently reference in the following endnotes: the **Congressional Research Service** and **Congressional Budget Office** are both *nonpartisan* research agencies of the Congress staffed by career professionals.

1   Sixteen Nobel Economists Sign Letter About Risks to the U.S. Economy of a Second Trump Presidency, https://www.documentcloud.org/documents/24777566-nobel-letter-final.

2   NBC News, *Border crossings fall to their lowest monthly number of the Joe Biden presidency*, at: https://www.nbcnews.com/investigations/border-crossings-fallen-lowest-monthly-number-Joe Biden-presidency-rcna159777; and https://www.nytimes.com/2024/07/16/us/politics/biden-border-immigration.html.

3   CNN, Trump wants to close the Department of Education, at: https://www.cnn.com/2023/09/13/politics/trump-department-of-education-states-2024/index.html.

4   Bloomberg at: https://www.bloomberg.com/graphics/Donald Trump-administration-conflicts/.

5   Project 2025 at: https://static.project2025.org/2025_MandateForLeadership_FULL.pdf.

6   CNN, *Trump claims not to know who is behind Project 2025. A CNN review found at least 140 people who worked for him are involved*, at: https://www.cnn.com/2024/07/11/politics/trump-allies-project-2025.

7   New York Times at: https://www.nytimes.com/2024/07/19/us/gunman-thomas-crooks-trump-shooting.html.

8   Associated Press (AP), *Yes, we're divided. But new AP-NORC poll shows Americans still agree on most core American values*, https://apnews.com/article/ap-poll-democracy-rights-freedoms-election-b1047da72551e13554a3959487e5181a.

9   Thomas Paine, *Common Sense* (January 1776), at: https://americainclass.org/wp-content/uploads/2023/08/Common-Sense-Full-Text.pdf.

10 Brown v. Board of Education, 347 U.S. 483, 495 (1954).

11 MLK at: https://www.americanrhetoric.com/speeches/mlkihaveadream.htm?ref=americanpurpose.com.

12 State of the State Courts: 2022 poll, National Center for State Courts, accessed at: https://www.ncsc.org/__data/assets/pdf_file/0019/85204/SSC_2022_Presentation.pdf.

13 Thomas Jefferson to the Abbé Arnoux, 19 July 1789, at: https://founders.archives.gov/documents/Jefferson/01-15-02-0275.

14 However, jury trials in civil cases are less common due to damage caps and binding arbitration. *See* Congressional Research Service, *The Right to a Jury Trial in Civil Cases* (Dec. 2022), https://crsreports.congress.gov/product/pdf/LSB/LSB10887.

15 Associated Press (AP), *Yes, we're divided. But new AP-NORC poll shows Americans still agree on most core American values*, at: https://apnews.com/article/ap-poll-democracy-rights-freedoms-election-b1047da72551e13554a3959487e5181a.

16   Declaration of Independence, at: https://www.archives.gov/founding-docs/declaration-transcript.

17   Associated Press (AP), *Yes, we're divided. But new AP-NORC poll shows Americans still agree on most core American values*, at: https://apnews.com/article/ap-poll-democracy-rights-freedoms-election-b1047da72551e13554a3959487e5181a.

18   Pew at: https://www.pewresearch.org/politics/2024/06/06/america-its-history-and-the-2024-election/.

19   Associated Press (AP), *Yes, we're divided. But new AP-NORC poll shows Americans still agree on most core American values*, at: https://apnews.com/article/ap-poll-democracy-rights-freedoms-election-b1047da72551e13554a3959487e5181a.

20   The extraordinary religious diversity of America is reflected in the Pew Research Center's Religious Landscape Studies, at: https://www.pewresearch.org/religious-landscape-study/database/.

21   From George Washington to the Hebrew Congregation in Newport, Rhode Island, 18 August 1790, at: https://founders.archives.gov/documents/Washington/05-06-02-0135.

22   *Griswold v. Connecticut*, 381 U.S. 479, 484 (1965). By a vote of 7–2, the Supreme Court invalidated a Connecticut prohibition on contraception on the grounds that it violated the "right to marital privacy" which is within the "penumbras" of specific guarantees of the Bill of Rights.

23   Gallup at: https://news.gallup.com/poll/642887/inflation-immigration-rank-among-top-issue-concerns.aspx.

24   U.S. Bureau of Labor Statistics, *Labor Force Statistics from the Current Population Survey: Unemployment Rate," select years 1948 to 2023*, at: https://data.bls.gov/timeseries/LNS14000000?years_option=all_years.

25   Fed Chair Powell said on August 23, 2024, that "inflation is on a sustainable path back to 2 percent," at: https://www.federalreserve.gov/newsevents/speech/powell20240823a.htm. See also Congressional Budget Office, *An Update to the Budget and Economic Outlook: 2024 to 2034* (June 2024) at: https://www.cbo.gov/publication/60039.

26   Statista at: https://www.statista.com/statistics/188185/percent-change-from-preceding-period-in-real-gdp-in-the-us/.

27   Fed Chair Powell said on Aug. 23, 2024, "the time has come for policy to adjust," which is Fed-speak for interest rates will begin dropping in September, at: https://www.federalreserve.gov/newsevents/speech/powell20240823a.htm.

28   U.S. Bureau of Labor Statistics, Labor Force Statistics from the Current Population Survey: Unemployment Rate," select years 1948 to 2023, at: https://data.bls.gov/timeseries/LNS14000000?years_option=all_years.

29   Politico at: https://www.politico.com/news/2024/08/02/rising-unemployment-biden-harris-00172442.

30 *See* FactCheck.org at: https://www.factcheck.org/2021/10/Donald Trumps-final-numbers/.

31 *See* FactCheck.org at: https://www.factcheck.org/2021/10/Donald Trumps-final-numbers/.

32 *See* FactCheck.org at: https://www.factcheck.org/2024/07/bidens-numbers-july-2024-update/.

33 *See* FactCheck.org at: https://www.factcheck.org/2021/10/trumps-final-numbers/.

34 *See* FactCheck.org at: https://www.factcheck.org/2024/07/bidens-numbers-july-2024-update/.

35 *Washington Post* at: https://www.washingtonpost.com/opinions/2024/07/18/trump-biden-economy-charts-compare/.

36 NBER at: https://www.nber.org/news/business-cycle-dating-committee-announcement-july-19-2021.

37 Congressional Budget Office at: https://www.cbo.gov/system/files/2022-05/57950-Outlook.pdf.

38 Congressional Budget Office at: https://www.cbo.gov/system/files/2023-02/58848-Outlook.pdf.

39 Congressional Budget Office at: https://www.cbo.gov/system/files/2024-06/60039-Outlook-2024.pdf.

40 BEA at: https://www.bea.gov/data/gdp/gross-domestic-product#.

41 World Bank (June 2024) at: https://openknowledge.worldbank.org/server/api/core/bitstreams/62a41ee3-b385-4f87-bd8b-1f413ef3e73d/content.

42 Federal Reserve at: https://fred.stlouisfed.org/series/BABATOTALSAUS.

43 White House at: https://www.whitehouse.gov/cea/written-materials/2021/06/17/why-the-pandemic-has-disrupted-supply-chains/; and the Congressional Budget Office at: https://www.cbo.gov/system/files/2020-05/56351-CBO-interim-projections.pdf.

44 Congressional Research Service, Inflation in the U.S. Economy: Causes and Policy Options, at: https://crsreports.congress.gov/product/pdf/R/R47273/4.

45 BLS at: https://www.bls.gov/charts/consumer-price-index/consumer-price-index-by-category-line-chart.htm.

46 NBC News, Why Russia's Ukraine invasion spiked energy prices, in 4 charts, https://www.nbcnews.com/news/world/why-russia-s-ukraine-invasion-spiked-energy-prices-4-charts-n1289799.

47 USDA, *The Ukraine Conflict and Other Factors Contributing to High Commodity Prices and Food Insecurity*, at: https://fas.usda.gov/data/ukraine-conflict-and-other-factors-contributing-high-commodity-prices-and-food-insecurity.

48 BLS at: https://www.bls.gov/charts/consumer-price-index/consumer-price-index-by-category-line-chart.htm.

49 Federal Reserve at: https://www.federalreserve.gov/faqs/money_12856.htm#.

50   BLS at: https://www.bls.gov/charts/consumer-price-index/consumer-price-index-by-category-line-chart.htm.

51   Federal Reserve Chair Jerome Powell said on Aug. 23, 2024, "the time has come for policy to adjust," which is Fed-speak for interest rates will begin dropping in September, at: https://www.federalreserve.gov/newsevents/speech/powell20240823a.htm.   .

52   Federal Reserve Bank of Minneapolis at: https://researchdatabase.minneapolisfed.org/downloads/sf268520m.

53   IRS at: https://www.irs.gov/newsroom/irs-provides-tax-inflation-adjustments-for-tax-year-2024.

54   Bloomberg at: https://www.bloomberg.com/news/articles/2024-06-13/Donald Trump-floats-tariffs-hikes-to-offset-some-income-tax-cuts; and CNN at: https://www.cnn.com/2024/08/15/politics/harris-trump-economy-policies-inflation/index.html.

55   CNN at: https://www.cnn.com/2024/02/04/politics/china-Donald Trump-tariffs-taiwan/index.html.

56   Council on Foreign Relations, *The Truth About Tariffs*, at: https://www.cfr.org/backgrounder/truth-about-tariffs#.

57   CNN, *How Trump's tariff plans could kill jobs and worsen inflation*, at: https://www.cnn.com/2024/04/11/economy/trump-tariffs-trade-jobs-inflation/index.html.

58   Interview with Time magazine at: https://time.com/6972022/donald-trump-transcript-2024-election/.

59   Harris-Walz at: https://mailchi.mp/press.kamalaharris.com/vice-president-harris-lays-out-agenda-to-lower-costs-for-american-families.

60   Congressional Research Service at: https://www.everycrsreport.com/files/20120723_R42020_51c47f5360876f3b2f92e4aca43661d736d1f158.pdf, and Congressional Budget Office at: https://www.cbo.gov/publication/54994.

61   Congressional Research Service at: https://sgp.fas.org/crs/natsec/RL33110.pdf; and Brown University at: https://watson.brown.edu/costsofwar/figures/2021/BudgetaryCosts.

62   Brown.edu at: https://watson.brown.edu/costsofwar/costs/human/military/killed#.

63   American Recovery and Reinvestment Act (ARPA) at: https://www.cbo.gov/publication/24988.

64   Budgetary Effects of COVID-19 legislation at: https://www.cbo.gov/publication/57343 and https://www.cbo.gov/system/files/2020-06/56403-CBO-covid-legislation.pdf; and Budgetary Effects of American Rescue Plan Act at: https://www.cbo.gov/publication/57056.

65   Congressional Budget Office at: https://www.cbo.gov/system/files/2024-03/59711-Long-Term-Outlook-2024.pdf.

66   See *Trillions: Federal Spending, Taxes, the U.S. Debt Ceiling, and Fiscal Law*, by Charles S. Konigsberg, available at: lexisnexis.com/trillions.

67   By contrast, total public debt, which topped $35 trillion on July 26, 2024, includes debt held by federal trust funds. Current numbers for debt-held-by-the-public and total public debt are available at: https://fiscaldata.treasury. gov/datasets/debt-to-the-penny/debt-to-the-penny.

68   Gross Domestic Product (GDP), is frequently used to measure the size of the economy. The components of GDP are consumption (both household and government), gross investment (both private and government), and net exports. See *Trillions* by Charles S. Konigsberg at www.lexisnexis.com/ trillions.

69   Budget of the U.S. Government for FY 2025, *Analytical Perspectives*, Table 21-1, at: https://www.whitehouse.gov/wp-content/uploads/2024/03/ap_21_ borrowing_fy2025.pdf.

70   FactCheck.org at: https://www.factcheck.org/2021/10/Donald Trumps-final-numbers/.

71   FactCheck.org at: https://www.factcheck.org/2024/07/bidens-numbers-july-2024-update/.

72   See NPR Morning Edition, Tax Cuts and the Deficit, at: https:// www.npr.org/2017/11/22/565881224/tax-cuts-and-the-deficit#:~:text=ZARROLI%3A%20Bernstein%20says%20there%27s%20 no%20evidence%20tax%20cuts,were%20followed%20by%20big%20 increases%20in%20the%20deficit.

73   Observations by the author on U.S. fiscal policy. *See* www.lexisnexis.com/ trillions by Charles S. Konigsberg.

74   Bipartisan Policy Center, *Restoring America's Future*, accessed at: https:// bipartisanpolicy.org/download/?file=/wp-content/uploads/2019/03/BPC-FINAL-REPORT-FOR-PRINTER-02-28-11.pdf. The author of this book, Charles S. Konigsberg, served as staff director of the Domenici-Rivlin Commission.

75   Congressional Budget Office, The Budget and Economic Outlook: 2024 to 2034, at: https://www.cbo.gov/system/files/2024-02/59710-Outlook-2024. pdf.

76   Congressional Budget Office at: https://www.cbo.gov/system/files/2024-03/59711-Long-Term-Outlook-2024.pdf.

77   Congressional Budget Office, The Budget and Economic Outlook: 2024 to 2034, at: https://www.cbo.gov/system/files/2024-02/59710-Outlook-2024. pdf.

78   Congressional Budget Office at: https://www.cbo.gov/system/files/2024-03/51119-2024-03-LTBO-budget.xlsx.

79   Congressional Budget Office, An Update to the Budget and Economic Outlook: 2024 to 2034 (June 2024), at: https://www.cbo.gov/system/ files/2024-06/60039-Outlook-2024.pdf.

80   USA Facts at: https://usafacts.org/articles/what-is-the-us-credit-rating/; and CNN at https://money.cnn.com/2011/08/05/news/economy/downgrade_ rumors/index.htm.

81   For example, see the Domenici-Rivlin Task Force, Bipartisan Policy Center, *Restoring America's Future*, accessed at: https://bipartisanpolicy.org/download/?file=/wp-content/uploads/2019/03/BPC-FINAL-REPORT-FOR-PRINTER-02-28-11.pdf. The author of this book, Charles S. Konigsberg, served as staff director of the Domenici-Rivlin Commission.

82   Tax Cuts and Jobs Act of 2017 at: https://www.congress.gov/bill/115th-congress/house-bill/1/text.

83   The $1.9 trillion estimate is over 10 years, and includes additional interest payments attributable to increased public debt, as well as marginal increases in economic growth due to the tax changes. *See* Congressional Budget Office, *The Effects of the 2017 Tax Act on CBO's Economic and Budget Projections*, Table B-3 at: https://www.cbo.gov/sites/default/files/115th-congress-2017-2018/reports/53651-outlook-appendixb.pdf..

84   These include provisions setting rates, the standard deduction, the estate tax exemption, the deduction for pass-through businesses, and the cap on state and local deductions. *See* Tax Policy Center, *2025 Promises to Be an Historic Year in Tax and Budget Policy*, at: https://www.taxpolicycenter.org/taxvox/buckle-2025-promises-be-historic-year-tax-and-budget-policy.

85   CNN, *Trump tells wealthy donors he wants to extend his 2017 tax cuts*, June 27, 2024, at: https://www.cnn.com/2024/04/10/politics/trump-2017-tax-cuts-rich/index.html.

86   Congressional Budget Office, *Budgetary Outcomes Under Alternative Assumptions About Spending and Revenues* (May 2024), Table 2, at: https://www.cbo.gov/system/files/2024-05/60114-Budgetary-Outcomes.pdf. This estimate includes revenue losses over 10 years attributable to extending the 2017 Tax Act's individual income tax provisions, estate and gift tax provisions, tax treatment of investment costs and other business tax provisions, plus additional interest payments due to the higher public debt.

87   CNN, *What voters need to know about Harris' and Trump's economic policy proposals*, at: https://www.cnn.com/2024/08/15/politics/harris-trump-economy-policies-inflation/index.html.

88   Analysis by the Urban-Brookings Tax Policy Center at: https://www.taxpolicycenter.org/model-estimates/make-certain-provisions-2017-tax-act-permanent-july-2024/t24-0025-make-certain.

89   CRFB at: https://www.crfb.org/blogs/donald-trumps-suggestion-end-taxation-social-security-benefits.

90   Bloomberg interview of Trump at: https://www.bloomberg.com/features/2024-trump-interview/; and Semafor at: https://finance.yahoo.com/news/trump-backs-corporate-tax-cut-024936583.html.

91   CNN, *Trump proposes eliminating taxes on tips at Las Vegas campaign rally*, at: https://www.cnn.com/2024/06/09/politics/donald-trump-nevada-rally/index.html.

92 Harris-Walz at: https://mailchi.mp/press.kamalaharris.com/vice-president-harris-lays-out-agenda-to-lower-costs-for-american-families.

93 Reuters, Kamala Harris proposes raising corporate tax rate to 28%, at: https://www.reuters.com/world/us/harris-calls-raising-us-corporate-tax-rate-28-percent-2024-08-19/.

94 CRFB at: https://www.crfb.org/blogs/kamala-harris-proposal-raise-corporate-tax-rate-28.

95 Harris-Walz Aug. 16, 2024 policy release at: https://mailchi.mp/press.kamalaharris.com/vice-president-harris-lays-out-agenda-to-lower-costs-for-american-families.

96 For estimates on the cost of these measures, without offsets, see the analysis by the Committee for a Responsible Federal Budget at: https://www.crfb.org/blogs/kamala-harris-agenda-lower-costs-american-families. However, the Harris-Walz Aug. 16, 2024, policy release states their "commitment to fiscal responsibility, including by asking the wealthiest Americans and largest corporations to pay their fair share—steps that will allow us to make necessary investments in the middle class, while also reducing the deficit and strengthening our fiscal health," https://mailchi.mp/press.kamalaharris.com/vice-president-harris-lays-out-agenda-to-lower-costs-for-american-families.

97 CNN, *Harris endorses eliminating taxes on tips*, at: https://www.cnn.com/2024/08/12/politics/taxes-on-tips-eliminate-proposal-harris/index.html; and CRFB at: https://www.crfb.org/blogs/kamala-harris-agenda-lower-costs-american-families.

98 Harris-Walz at: https://mailchi.mp/press.kamalaharris.com/vice-president-harris-lays-out-agenda-to-lower-costs-for-american-families.

99 Harris-Walz at: https://mailchi.mp/press.kamalaharris.com/vice-president-harris-lays-out-agenda-to-lower-costs-for-american-families.

100 Harris-Walz at: https://mailchi.mp/press.kamalaharris.com/vice-president-harris-lays-out-agenda-to-lower-costs-for-american-families.

101 Harris-Walz release, Aug. 16, 2024 at: https://mailchi.mp/press.kamalaharris.com/vice-president-harris-lays-out-agenda-to-lower-costs-for-american-families.

102 Fiscal Responsibility Act at: https://www.congress.gov/bill/118th-congress/house-bill/3746. For a full explanation of the statutory limit on the public debt ("debt ceiling") see *Trillions: Federal Spending, Taxes, the U.S. Debt Ceiling, and Fiscal Law* at: www.lexisnexis.com/trillions.

103 Politico at: https://www.politico.com/video/2023/05/10/Donald Trump-u-s-might-as-well-default-on-debt-910431.

104 Accessed at: https://www.documentcloud.org/documents/24777566-nobel-letter-final.

105 Gallup at: https://news.gallup.com/poll/642887/inflation-immigration-rank-among-top-issue-concerns.aspx.

106 **Unless otherwise noted,** the content and quotations in this section are derived from a historical timeline at: https://www.history.com/ topics/immigration/immigration-united-states-timeline. *See also,* Pew Research Center report at: https://www.pewresearch.org/race-and-ethnicity/2015/09/28/chapter-1-the-nations-immigration-laws-1920-to-today/.

107 National Archives at: https://www.archives.gov/milestone-documents/ chinese-exclusion-act.

108 "First-generation immigrants" are the first foreign-born family members to gain citizenship or permanent residency in the country, United States Census Bureau, https://www.census.gov/topics/population/foreign-born/about.html.

109 *See* https://www.history.com/this-day-in-history/immigration-act-passed-over-wilsons-veto.

110 See https://history.state.gov/milestones/1921-1936/immigration-act.

111 *See* https://2009-2017.state.gov/j/prm/releases/factsheets/2015/244058.htm. *See also,* Pew Research Center report at: https://www.pewresearch.org/race-and-ethnicity/2015/09/28/chapter-1-the-nations-immigration-laws-1920-to-today/.

112 USCIS at: https://www.uscis.gov/laws-and-policy/legislation/immigration-and-nationality-act.

113 *See* https://immigrationhistory.org/item/1986-immigration-reform-and-control-act/.

114 What we know about unauthorized immigrants living in the U.S. (July 2024), at: https://www.pewresearch.org/short-reads/2024/07/22/what-we-know-about-unauthorized-immigrants-living-in-the-us/.

115 Pew Research Center, Migrant encounters at the U.S.-Mexico border hit a record high at the end of 2023, at: https://www.pewresearch.org/short-reads/2024/02/15/migrant-encounters-at-the-us-mexico-border-hit-a-record-high-at-the-end-of-2023/.

116 *Senate Republicans block bipartisan border deal and foreign aid package following months of negotiations,* https://www.cnn.com/2024/02/07/politics/ senate-border-ukraine-israel-aid-vote/index.htm.

117 *Border bill fails in Senate for second time,* https://www.cnn.com/2024/05/23/ politics/senate-border-bill-vote/index.html.

118 White House fact sheet at: https://www.whitehouse.gov/briefing-room/ statements-releases/2024/06/04/fact-sheet-president-Joe Biden-announces-new-actions-to-secure-the-border/.

119 CBS News at: https://www.cbsnews.com/news/unlawful-border-crossings-drop-5th-straight-month-lowest-level-since-september-2020/.

120 This explanation is sourced from *How the United States Immigration System Works,* by the American Immigration Council, a nonprofit established by the American Immigration Lawyers Association, at: https://www. americanimmigrationcouncil.org/research/how-united-states-immigration-

system-works; and *Primer on U.S. Immigration Policy*, by the Congressional Research Service, at: https://crsreports.congress.gov/product/pdf/R/R45020.

121 CFR, *The U.S. Immigration Debate*, at: https://www.cfr.org/backgrounder/us-immigration-debate-0.

122 CFR, *The U.S. Immigration Debate*, at: https://www.cfr.org/backgrounder/us-immigration-debate-0.

123 USCIS at: https://www.uscis.gov/family/family-of-us-citizens.

124 CFR, *The U.S. Immigration Debate*, at: https://www.cfr.org/backgrounder/us-immigration-debate-0.

125 CFR, *The U.S. Immigration Debate*, at: https://www.cfr.org/backgrounder/us-immigration-debate-0.

126 CFR, *The U.S. Immigration Debate*, at: https://www.cfr.org/backgrounder/us-immigration-debate-0.

127 CFR, *The U.S. Immigration Debate*, at: https://www.cfr.org/backgrounder/us-immigration-debate-0.

128 USA.gov at: https://www.usa.gov/green-card-lottery.

129 Migration Policy Institute at: https://www.migrationpolicy.org/content/explainer-how-us-legal-immigration-system-works.

130 USCIS at: https://www.uscis.gov/citizenship/apply-for-citizenship.

131 CFR, *The U.S. Immigration Debate*, at: https://www.cfr.org/backgrounder/us-immigration-debate-0.

132 USCIS at: https://www.uscis.gov/DACA.

133 Unless otherwise indicated, this section is based on information provided by PolitiFact, a project of the nonpartisan Poynter Institute, accessed at: https://www.politifact.com/article/2022/sep/06/surprising-number-americans-believe-these-false-cl/;

134 For the latest statistics on immigrants becoming U.S. citizens, see: https://www.uscis.gov/citizenship-resource-center/naturalization-statistics. For an in-depth analysis of the most common myths about immigration, see https://www.libertarianism.org/sites/libertarianism.org/files/2021-04/The%20Most%20Common%20Arguments%20Against%20Immigration%20and%20Why%20They%27re%20Wrong.pdf?hsCtaTracking=5b590920-b88a-4641-ba7b-5fdc41e9a266%7Cba17362a-c667-46dd-9170-b112363474e3.

135 Congressional Budget Office, *The Budget and Economic Outlook: 2024 to 2034*, at: https://www.cbo.gov/publication/59946.

136 CFR, *The U.S. Immigration Debate*, at: https://www.cfr.org/backgrounder/us-immigration-debate-0.

137 Congressional Budget Office, *The Foreign-Born Population, the U.S. Economy, and the Federal Budget*, accessed at: https://www.cbo.gov/publication/59046#_idTextAnchor010.

138 Congressional Budget Office, *The Budget and Economic Outlook: 2024 to 2034*, at: https://www.cbo.gov/publication/59946

139 Dept. of Justice, *Comparing Crime Rates Between Undocumented Immigrants, Legal Immigrants, and Native-born U.S. citizens in Texas*, accessed at: https://www.ojp.gov/library/publications/comparing-crime-rates-between-undocumented-immigrants-legal-immigrants-and.

140 Congressional Research Service, *Illicit Drug Smuggling Between Ports of Entry and Border Barriers*, R46218, accessed at: https://crsreports.congress.gov/product/pdf/R/R46218/2.

141 *List of countries and dependencies by population density*, accessed at: https://en.wikipedia.org/wiki/List_of_countries_and_dependencies_by_population_density.

142 CFR, *The U.S. Immigration Debate*, at: https://www.cfr.org/backgrounder/us-immigration-debate-0.

143 Ronald Reagan, Statement on Signing the Immigration Reform and Control Act of 1986, at: https://www.reaganlibrary.gov/archives/speech/statement-signing-immigration-reform-and-control-act-1986.

144 Donald Trump interview by Time Magazine (April 2024), at: https://time.com/6972022/donald-Donald Trump-transcript-2024-election/.

145 Brennan Center for Justice, *The Posse Comitatus Act Explained* at: https://www.brennancenter.org/our-work/research-reports/posse-comitatus-act-explained.

146 White House at: https://www.whitehouse.gov/briefing-room/statements-releases/2021/01/20/fact-sheet-president-Joe Biden-sends-immigration-bill-to-congress-as-part-of-his-commitment-to-modernize-our-immigration-system/.

147 Pew at: https://www.pewresearch.org/politics/2024/06/06/immigration-attitudes-and-the-2024-election/.

148 White House at: https://www.whitehouse.gov/briefing-room/statements-releases/2024/01/26/statement-from-president-joe-Joe Biden-on-the-bipartisan-senate-border-security-negotiations/.

149 CNN at: https://www.cnn.com/2015/07/29/politics/donald-Donald Trump-immigration-plan-healthcare-flip-flop/index.html.

150 NBC News at: https://www.nbcnews.com/politics/congress/republicans-kill-border-bill-sign-Donald Trumps-strength-mcconnells-waning-in-rcna137477.

151 Kamala Harris in Aug. 22, 2024 convention speech: "I refuse to play politics with our security. Here is my pledge to you: As President, I will bring back the bipartisan border security bill that he killed. And I will sign it into law," at: https://abcnews.go.com/Politics/read-kamala-harris-full-speech-democratic-national-convention/story?id=113086031.

152 White House at: https://www.whitehouse.gov/briefing-room/statements-releases/2024/06/04/fact-sheet-president-Joe Biden-announces-new-actions-to-secure-the-border/.

153 CBS News at: https://www.cbsnews.com/news/unlawful-border-crossings-drop-5th-straight-month-lowest-level-since-september-2020/.

154 Joe Biden statement (July 17, 2021) at: https://www.whitehouse.gov/briefing-room/statements-releases/2021/07/17/statement-by-president-joe-Joe Biden-on-daca-and-legislation-for-dreamers/.

155 NPR: *Supreme Court Rules for DREAMers, Against Donald Trump*, at: https://www.npr.org/2020/06/18/829858289/supreme-court-upholds-daca-in-blow-to-Donald Trump-administration.

156 White House at: https://www.whitehouse.gov/briefing-room/statements-releases/2021/05/03/statement-by-president-joe-biden-on-refugee-admissions/.

157 CBS News at: https://www.cbsnews.com/news/Donald Trump-administration-refugee-resettlement-cap-historic-low/.

158 CFR, *How Does the U.S. Refugee System Work*, at: https://www.cfr.org/backgrounder/how-does-us-refugee-system-work-Donald Trump-Joe Biden-afghanistan#chapter-title-0-4.

159 C-Span at: https://www.c-span.org/video/?c5098439/donald-Donald Trump-illegal-immigrants-poisoning-blood-country.

160 NBC News, *Donald Trump doubles down on immigrant blood remark*, at: https://www.nbcnews.com/politics/donald-Donald Trump/Donald Trump-doubles-immigrant-blood-remark-says-never-read-mein-kampf-rcna130535.

161 NBC News, *Donald Trump says immigrants are 'poisoning the blood of our country.' Joe Biden campaign likens comments to Hitler*, at: https://www.nbcnews.com/politics/2024-election/Donald Trump-says-immigrants-are-poisoning-blood-country-Joe Biden-campaign-liken-rcna130141. *See also*, https://www.msn.com/en-us/news/politics/fact-check-did-donald-trump-quote-hitler-s-mein-kampf-in-his-speech-dangerous-remarks-on-immigrants-explored/ar-AA1lIIeu.

162 White House, *Biden-Harris Administration Releases First-Ever U.S. National Strategy to Counter Antisemitism* (May 25, 2023), at: https://www.whitehouse.gov/briefing-room/statements-releases/2023/05/25/fact-sheet-Joe Biden-harris-administration-releases-first-ever-u-s-national-strategy-to-counter-antisemitism/.

163 NPR, *Joe Biden White House Aims to Advance Racial Equity with Executive Actions*, at: https://www.npr.org/sections/president-Joe Biden-takes-office/2021/01/26/960725707/Joe Biden-aims-to-advance-racial-equity-with-executive-actions.

164 White House, *Biden-Harris Administration Releases First-Ever U.S. National Strategy to Counter Antisemitism* (May 25, 2023), at: https://www.whitehouse.gov/briefing-room/statements-releases/2023/05/25/fact-sheet-Joe Biden-harris-administration-releases-first-ever-u-s-national-strategy-to-counter-antisemitism/.

165 Associated Press (AP), *Yes, we're divided. But new AP-NORC poll shows Americans still agree on most core American values*, https://

apnews.com/article/ap-poll-democracy-rights-freedoms-election-b1047da72551e13554a3959487e5181a.

166 FactCheck.org at: https://www.factcheck.org/2024/07/bidens-numbers-july-2024-update/.

167 FactCheck.org at: https://www.factcheck.org/2024/07/bidens-numbers-july-2024-update/.

168 U.S. Bureau of Labor Statistics, *Labor Force Statistics from the Current Population Survey: Unemployment Rate, select years 1948 to 2023*, at: https://data.bls.gov/timeseries/LNS14000000?years_option=all_years.

169 Fed Chair Powell said on Aug. 23, 2024, "the time has come for policy to adjust," which is Fed-speak for interest rates will begin dropping in September, https://www.federalreserve.gov/newsevents/speech/powell20240823a.htm.

170 Harris-Walz at: https://mailchi.mp/press.kamalaharris.com/vice-president-harris-lays-out-agenda-to-lower-costs-for-american-families.

171 Harris-Walz at: https://mailchi.mp/press.kamalaharris.com/vice-president-harris-lays-out-agenda-to-lower-costs-for-american-families.

172 KFF at: https://www.kff.org/affordable-care-act/issue-brief/how-the-american-rescue-plan-act-affects-subsidies-for-marketplace-shoppers-and-people-who-are-; and Harris-Walz at: https://mailchi.mp/press.kamalaharris.com/vice-president-harris-lays-out-agenda-to-lower-costs-for-american-families.

173 Harris-Walz release, Aug. 16, 2024 at: https://mailchi.mp/press.kamalaharris.com/vice-president-harris-lays-out-agenda-to-lower-costs-for-american-families.

174 Harris-Walz release, Aug. 16, 2024 at: https://mailchi.mp/press.kamalaharris.com/vice-president-harris-lays-out-agenda-to-lower-costs-for-american-families.

175 Harris-Walz release, Aug. 16, 2024 at: https://mailchi.mp/press.kamalaharris.com/vice-president-harris-lays-out-agenda-to-lower-costs-for-american-families.

176 White House, *President Joe Biden Takes New Steps to Lower Prescription Drug and Health Care Costs* (March 2024), at: https://www.whitehouse.gov/briefing-room/statements-releases/2024/03/06/fact-sheet-president-Joe Biden-takes-new-steps-to-lower-prescription-drug-and-health-care-costs-expand-access-to-health-care-and-protect-consumers/.

177 KFF at: https://www.kff.org/medicare/issue-brief/millions-of-people-with-medicare-will-benefit-from-the-new-out-of-pocket-drug-spending-cap-over-time/.

178 Harris-Walz at: https://mailchi.mp/press.kamalaharris.com/vice-president-harris-lays-out-agenda-to-lower-costs-for-american-families.

179 White House at: https://www.whitehouse.gov/briefing-room/statements-releases/2024/06/11/fact-sheet-vice-president-harris-announces-proposal-to-

prohibit-medical-bills-from-being-included-on-credit-reports-and-calls-on-states-and-localities-to-take-further-actions-to-reduce-medical-debt/#.

180 Harris-Walz at: https://mailchi.mp/press.kamalaharris.com/vice-president-harris-lays-out-agenda-to-lower-costs-for-american-families.

181 Forbes at: https://www.forbes.com/sites/adamminsky/2024/06/20/trump-knocks-bidens-vile-student-loan-forgiveness-plans-suggests-reversal/.

182 Department of Education at: https://www.ed.gov/news/press-releases/biden-harris-administration-announces-additional-77-billion-approved-student-debt-relief-160000-borrowers.

183 Politico at: https://subscriber.politicopro.com/article/eenews/2024/07/29/biden-balanced-unions-and-climate-harris-could-too-in-her-own-way-00171430; and White House at: https://www.whitehouse.gov/briefing-room/statements-releases/2024/07/02/fact-sheet-president-biden-announces-new-actions-to-protect-workers-and-communities-from-extreme-weather/.

184 FactCheck.org at: https://www.factcheck.org/2021/10/trumps-final-numbers/.

185 CNN, *Trump tells wealthy donors he wants to extend his 2017 tax cuts*, June 27, 2024, at: https://www.cnn.com/2024/04/10/politics/trump-2017-tax-cuts-rich/index.html.

186 TPC at: https://www.taxpolicycenter.org/model-estimates/make-certain-provisions-2017-tax-act-permanent-july-2024/t24-0025-make-certain; and CNN at: https://www.cnn.com/2024/07/08/politics/trump-tax-cuts-tcja-wealthy-benefit/index.html.

187 Bloomberg, *Trump Floats Tariff Hikes to Offset Some Income Tax Cuts*, at: https://www.bloomberg.com/news/articles/2024-06-13/trump-floats-tariffs-hikes-to-offset-some-income-tax-cuts; and CNN, *What voters need to know about Harris' and Trump's economic policy proposals,* at: https://www.cnn.com/2024/08/15/politics/harris-trump-economy-policies-inflation/index.html.

188 Council on Foreign Relations, *The Truth About Tariffs*, at: https://www.cfr.org/backgrounder/truth-about-tariffs#:~:text=Tariffs%20are%20a%20form%20of%20tax%20applied%20on,to%20retaliate%20against%20other%20countries%E2%80%99%20unfair%20trade%20practices; and CNN, *How Trump's tariff plans could kill jobs and worsen inflation*, at: https://www.cnn.com/2024/04/11/economy/trump-tariffs-trade-jobs-inflation/index.html#.

189 CNN, *How Trump's tariff plans could kill jobs and worsen inflation*, at: https://www.cnn.com/2024/04/11/economy/trump-tariffs-trade-jobs-inflation/index.html#.

190 Interview with Time magazine at: https://time.com/6972022/donald-trump-transcript-2024-election/.

191 Nobel letter accessed at: https://www.documentcloud.org/documents/24777566-nobel-letter-final.

192 CNN, *Donald Trump suggests he's open to cuts to Medicare and Social*

Security after attacking primary rivals over the issue, at: https://www.cnn.com/2024/03/11/politics/Donald Trump-entitlements-social-security-medicare/index.html.

193 For an explanation of taxes on Social Security benefits, see CRFB at: https://www.crfb.org/blogs/donald-trumps-suggestion-end-taxation-social-security-benefits.

194 CRFB at: https://www.crfb.org/blogs/donald-trumps-suggestion-end-taxation-social-security-benefits.

195 Donald Trump interview by Time Magazine (April 2024), at: https://time.com/6972022/donald-Donald Trump-transcript-2024-election/.

196 KFF at: https://www.kff.org/interactive/proposals-to-replace-the-affordable-care-act/.

197 PolitiFact at: https://www.politifact.com/truth-o-meter/promises/trumpometer/promise/1388/repeal-obamacare/.

198 Congressional Budget Office at: https://www.cbo.gov/publication/52752.

199 Forbes at: https://www.forbes.com/sites/adamminsky/2024/06/20/trump-knocks-bidens-vile-student-loan-forgiveness-plans-suggests-reversal/.

200 Social Security Administration, *Fast Facts 2023*, at: https://www.ssa.gov/policy/docs/chartbooks/fast_facts/2023/fast_facts23.pdf.

201 Congressional Research Service, *Social Security's Funding Shortfall* (May 2023) at: https://crsreports.congress.gov/product/pdf/IF/IF10522.

202 *2024 Annual Report of the Board of Trustees of the Federal Old-Age and Survivors Insurance and Federal Disability Insurance Trust Funds,* at: https://www.ssa.gov/OACT/TR/2024/index.html.

203 CRFB at: https://www.crfb.org/blogs/donald-trumps-suggestion-end-taxation-social-security-benefits.

204 CRFB at: https://www.crfb.org/blogs/donald-trumps-suggestion-end-taxation-social-security-benefits.

205 Report of the National Commission on Social Security Reform, at: https://www.ssa.gov/history/reports/gspan.html.

206 Bipartisan Policy Center, *Restoring America's Future,* accessed at: https://bipartisanpolicy.org/download/?file=/wp-content/uploads/2019/03/BPC-FINAL-REPORT-FOR-PRINTER-02-28-11.pdf.

207 Social Security Administration, *Effects of Unauthorized Immigration on the Actuarial Status of the Social Security Trust Funds* (April 2013), at: https://www.ssa.gov/oact/NOTES/pdf_notes/note151.pdf.

208 CNN, *Donald Trump suggests he's open to cuts to Medicare and Social Security after attacking primary rivals over the issue,* at: https://www.cnn.com/2024/03/11/politics/Donald Trump-entitlements-social-security-medicare/index.html.

209 For an explanation of taxation of Social Security benefits, see CRFB at: https://www.crfb.org/blogs/donald-trumps-suggestion-end-taxation-social-security-benefits.

210 CRFB at: https://www.crfb.org/blogs/donald-trumps-suggestion-end-

taxation-social-security-benefits.

211 Donald Trump interview by Time Magazine (April 2024), at: https://time.
com/6972022/donald-Donald Trump-transcript-2024-election/.

212 Yahoo Finance at: https://finance.yahoo.com/news/joe-biden-wants-save-
social-084200449.html.

213 Census at: https://www.census.gov/library/publications/2023/demo/p60-281.
html#.

214 KFF at: https://www.kff.org/medicaid/issue-brief/medicaid-a-primer/; and
Census at: https://www.census.gov/library/publications/2023/demo/p60-281.
html#.

215 "Amyotrophic lateral sclerosis (ALS), also known as Lou Gehrig's disease,
is a neurological disorder that affects the nerve cells in the brain and spinal
cord that control voluntary muscle movement and breathing," https://www.
ninds.nih.gov/health-information/disorders/amyotrophic-lateral-sclerosis-
als#.

216 KFF at: https://www.kff.org/medicare/issue-brief/an-overview-
of-medicare/#, and Census at: https://www.census.gov/library/
publications/2023/demo/p60-281.html#.

217 Medicaid.gov at: https://www.medicaid.gov/chip/eligibility/index.html.

218 KFF at: https://files.kff.org/attachment/The-Uninsured-and-the-ACA-A-
Primer-Key-Facts-about-Health-Insurance-and-the-Uninsured-amidst-
Changes-to-the-Affordable-Care-Act.

219 Congressional Research Service at: https://crsreports.congress.gov/product/
pdf/IF/IF10555.

220 *TRICARE 101* at: https://tricare.mil/Plans/New#:~:text=What%20
is%20TRICARE%3F%20TRICARE%20is%20the%20uniformed%20
services,family%20members%2C%20survivors%2C%20and%20certain%20
former%20spouses%20worldwide.

221 Congressional Research Service at: https://crsreports.congress.gov/product/
pdf/RS/RS22483.

222 IHS at: https://www.ihs.gov/aboutihs/.

223 CMS Fast Facts at: https://data.cms.gov/sites/default/files/2024-03/
CMSFastFactsMar2024_508.pdf.

224 KFF at: https://www.kff.org/medicare/issue-brief/medicare-advantage-in-
2024-enrollment-update-and-key-trends/#.

225 CBPP at: https://www.cbpp.org/research/medicare-is-not-bankrupt#.

226 Social Security Administration, *Fast Facts 2023*, at: https://www.ssa.gov/
policy/docs/chartbooks/fast_facts/2023/fast_facts23.pdf.

227 Paul N. Van De Water, *Medicare Is Not Bankrupt*, at: https://www.cbpp.
org/research/medicare-is-not-bankrupt#. Up to 85 percent of a recipient's
benefits are subject to the individual income tax, depending on the recipient's
overall income. The Congressional Budget Office estimated that about half
of all Social Security beneficiaries owed some income tax on their benefits.

CBO at: https://www.cbo.gov/publication/49948.

228 2024 Medicare Trustees Report, at https://www.cms.gov/oact/tr/2024.

229 Congressional Budget Office, *The Long-Term Budget Outlook*, at: https://www.cbo.gov/system/files/2024-03/59711-Long-Term-Outlook-2024.pdf.

230 Social Security Administration, *Effects of Unauthorized Immigration on the Actuarial Status of the Social Security Trust Funds* (April 2013), at: https://www.ssa.gov/oact/NOTES/pdf_notes/note151.pdf.

231 For an explanation of taxes on Social Security benefits, see CRFB at: https://www.crfb.org/blogs/donald-trumps-suggestion-end-taxation-social-security-benefits.

232 CRFB at: https://www.crfb.org/blogs/donald-trumps-suggestion-end-taxation-social-security-benefits.

233 Donald Trump interview by Time Magazine (April 2024), at: https://time.com/6972022/donald-Donald Trump-transcript-2024-election/.

234 Washington Post at: https://www.washingtonpost.com/news/powerpost/paloma/the-health-202/2018/02/09/the-health-202-republicans-kill-obamacare-s-controversial-death-panel/5a7c601d30fb041c3c7d76c7/.

235 The Dispatch at: https://www.yahoo.com/news/did-aca-accomplish-064600422.html?fr=sycsrp_catchall.

236 KFF at: https://www.kff.org/medicare/issue-brief/millions-of-people-with-medicare-will-benefit-from-the-new-out-of-pocket-drug-spending-cap-over-time/.

237 KFF at: https://www.kff.org/compare-2024-candidates-health-care-policy/?utm_campaign=KFF-Health-Policy-101.

238 White House, *President Joe Biden Takes New Steps to Lower Prescription Drug and Health Care Costs* (March 2024), at: https://www.whitehouse.gov/briefing-room/statements-releases/2024/03/06/fact-sheet-president-Joe Biden-takes-new-steps-to-lower-prescription-drug-and-health-care-costs-expand-access-to-health-care-and-protect-consumers/.

239 Harris-Walz at: https://mailchi.mp/press.kamalaharris.com/vice-president-harris-lays-out-agenda-to-lower-costs-for-american-families.

240 KFF at: https://www.kff.org/medicare/issue-brief/explaining-the-prescription-drug-provisions-in-the-inflation-reduction-act/#.

241 The ACA was enacted in two parts: The Patient Protection and Affordable Care Act was signed into law on March 23, 2010, which was amended by the Health Care and Education Reconciliation Act on March 30, 2010.

242 KFF, *The Uninsured and the ACA: A Primer - Key Facts about Health Insurance and the Uninsured amidst Changes to the Affordable Care Act*, at: https://www.kff.org/uninsured/report/the-uninsured-and-the-aca-a-primer-key-facts-about-health-insurance-and-the-uninsured-amidst-changes-to-the-affordable-care-act/.

243 ASPE Issue Brief, DHHS, *Health Insurance Coverage and the Affordable Care Act, 2010-2016*, at: https://web.archive.org/web/20211205091604/

https://aspe.hhs.gov/sites/default/files/migrated_legacy_files//142146/
ACA2010-2016.pdf.

244 In *National Federation of Independent Business v. Sebelius*, 567 U.S. 519
(2012), the Supreme Court ruled that states could not be forced to participate
in the ACA's Medicaid expansion but upheld the ACA as a whole.

245 Healthcare.gov at: https://www.healthcare.gov/glossary/federal-poverty-
level-fpl/.

246 Healthcare.gov at: https://www.healthcare.gov/young-adults/children-
under-26/; and White House at: https://obamawhitehouse.archives.gov/sites/
default/files/rss_viewer/fact_sheet_young_adults_may10.pdf

247 KFF at: https://www.kff.org/interactive/proposals-to-replace-the-affordable-
care-act/.

248 PolitiFact.com at: https://www.politifact.com/truth-o-meter/promises/
trumpometer/promise/1388/repeal-obamacare/.

249 Congressional Budget Office at: https://www.cbo.gov/publication/52752.

250 CNN at: https://www.cnn.com/2018/07/10/politics/obamacare-trump/index.
html.

251 CNN at: https://www.cnn.com/2018/07/10/politics/obamacare-trump/index.
html.

252 CNN at: https://money.cnn.com/2017/10/12/news/economy/trump-
obamacare-enrollment/index.html.

253 CNN at: https://money.cnn.com/2017/10/13/news/economy/trump-
obamacare-subsidies/index.html.

254 KFF at: https://www.kff.org/affordable-care-act/issue-brief/how-the-loss-of-
cost-sharing-subsidy-payments-is-affecting-2018-premiums/.

255 CNN, *Donald Trump had 4 years to remake Obamacare. Here's what he did*,
at: https://www.cnn.com/2024/04/12/politics/obamacare-Donald Trump-
administration/index.html.

256 KFF at: https://www.kff.org/private-insurance/issue-brief/navigator-funding-
restored-in-federal-marketplace-states-for-2022/.

257 CNN, *Donald Trump had 4 years to remake Obamacare. Here's what he did*,
at: https://www.cnn.com/2024/04/12/politics/obamacare-Donald Trump-
administration/index.html and KFF at: https://www.kff.org/state-category/
affordable-care-act/health-insurance-marketplaces/.

258 Morning Consult, *Obamacare Has Become Even More Popular Over Joe
Biden's Presidency*, at: https://pro.morningconsult.com/analysis/obamacare-
polling-popularity.

259 KFF at: https://www.kff.org/affordable-care-act/issue-brief/how-the-
american-rescue-plan-act-affects-subsidies-for-marketplace-shoppers-and-
people-who-are- and Harris-Walz at: https://mailchi.mp/press.kamalaharris.
com/vice-president-harris-lays-out-agenda-to-lower-costs-for-american-
families.

260 KFF at: https://www.kff.org/affordable-care-act/issue-brief/navigating-the-family-glitch-fix-hurdles-for-consumers-with-employer-sponsored-coverage/.

261 Harris-Walz at: https://mailchi.mp/press.kamalaharris.com/vice-president-harris-lays-out-agenda-to-lower-costs-for-american-families.

262 CMS at: https://www.federalregister.gov/documents/2024/05/10/2024-08273/medicare-and-medicaid-programs-minimum-staffing-standards-for-long-term-care-facilities-and-medicaid.

263 White House at: https://www.whitehouse.gov/briefing-room/statements-releases/2024/06/11/fact-sheet-vice-president-harris-announces-proposal-to-prohibit-medical-bills-from-being-included-on-credit-reports-and-calls-on-states-and-localities-to-take-further-actions-to-reduce-medical-debt/#.

264 Harris-Walz at: https://mailchi.mp/press.kamalaharris.com/vice-president-harris-lays-out-agenda-to-lower-costs-for-american-families.

265 U.S. Mission at: https://geneva.usmission.gov/2021/01/21/dr-anthony-s-fauci-remarks-at-the-who-executive-board-meeting/.

266 Poll by the Bipartisan Policy Center, National Housing Conference, and Morning Consult at: https://bipartisanpolicy.org/blog/opinions-on-housing-affordability-poll/.

267 FDR Library at: https://www.fdrlibrary.org/housing#:~:text=With%20the%20major%20concerns%20of,and%20on%2060%2Dyear%20terms.

268 USA.gov at: https://www.hud.gov/topics/housing_choice_voucher_program_section_8.

269 USA.gov at: https://www.usa.gov/public-housing.

270 USDA at: https://www.rd.usda.gov/programs-services/all-programs/housing-programs.

271 VA at: https://www.benefits.va.gov/homeloans/index.asp.

272 VA at: https://www.va.gov/homeless/hud-vash.asp.

273 Treasury at: https://home.treasury.gov/policy-issues/coronavirus/assistance-for-state-local-and-tribal-governments/homeowner-assistance-fund.

274 **The source for the following bullet points** is a Harris-Walz release, Aug. 16, 2024 at: https://mailchi.mp/press.kamalaharris.com/vice-president-harris-lays-out-agenda-to-lower-costs-for-american-families.

275 **The source for the following bullet points is** ABA at: https://www.americanbar.org/groups/crsj/publications/human_rights_magazine_home/vol--44--no-2--housing/the-trump-administration-s-impact-on-public-and-assisted-housing/.

276 States have a variety of exceptions for various medical, religious or philosophical reasons. *See* CDC at: https://www.cdc.gov/phlp/docs/school-vaccinations.pdf.

277 MSN News at: https://www.msn.com/en-us/news/politics/Donald Trump-vows-historic-cut-to-education-department-in-second-term/ar-BB1oIyRi.

278 CNN at: https://www.cnn.com/2023/09/13/politics/trump-department-of-education-states-2024/index.html.

279 Department of Education at: https://www2.ed.gov/about/overview/budget/budget25/summary/25summary.pdf.

280 Department of Education at: https://www2.ed.gov/about/overview/budget/budget25/summary/25summary.pdf.

281 CDC at https://www.cdc.gov/vaccines/imz-managers/guides-pubs/downloads/vacc_mandates_chptr13.pdf.

282 *Jacobson v. Massachusetts*, 197 U.S. 11 (1905).

283 CDC at: https://www.cdc.gov/vaccines/imz-managers/guides-pubs/downloads/vacc_mandates_chptr13.pdf.

284 **Source for the quotes in this subsection, unless otherwise specified is** World Health Organization at: https://www.who.int/news-room/commentaries/detail/embrace-the-facts-about-vaccines-not-the-myths.

285 AARP at: https://www.aarp.org/health/drugs-supplements/info-2020/covid-vaccine-myths.html.

286 AARP at: https://www.aarp.org/health/drugs-supplements/info-2020/covid-vaccine-myths.html.

287 AARP at: https://www.aarp.org/health/drugs-supplements/info-2020/covid-vaccine-myths.html.

288 CDC at: https://www.cdc.gov/media/releases/2022/s0318-COVID-19-vaccines-protect.html.

289 CDC at: https://www.cdc.gov/washington/testimony/2020/t20200702.htm.

290 PBS News Hour at: https://www.pbs.org/newshour/show/Donald Trump-vows-to-defund-schools-requiring-vaccines-for-students-if-hes-reelected; and Politico, https://www.politico.com/news/2024/06/09/Donald Trump-anti-vaccine-mandates-00162360.

291 NPR at: https://www.npr.org/sections/health-shots/2022/01/18/1073292913/a-year-in-experts-assess-Joe Bidens-hits-and-misses-on-handling-the-pandemic.

292 GAO, *Defense Production Act*, GAO-21-108, at: https://www.gao.gov/products/gao-21-108#:~:text=What%20GAO%20Found,domestic%20production%20of%20medical%20supplies.

293 CNN, *Trump wants to close the Department of Education*, at: https://www.cnn.com/2023/09/13/politics/trump-department-of-education-states-2024/index.html.

294 New York Times, *Schools Got a Record $190 billion in Pandemic Aid*, at: https://www.nytimes.com/2024/06/26/us/pandemic-aid-recovery-schools.html.

295 ABC News at: https://abcnews.go.com/Politics/education-policy-harris-trump-differ-12-higher-education/story?id=112977887.

296 Kamala Harris at: https://www.facebook.com/photo.php?fbid=10153861515

712923&id=24413227922&set=a.391094312922.

297 Congressional Research Service at: https://crsreports.congress.gov/product/pdf/IF/IF12136.

298 Dept. of Education at.: https://studentaid.gov/announcements-events/covid-19#payment-pause-and-0-interest.

299 Congressional Research Service at: https://crsreports.congress.gov/product/pdf/IF/IF12136.

300 Student Debt Timeline at: https://www.investopedia.com/student-debt-timeline-7112128.

301 *Biden v. Nebraska* (No. 22-506, June 30, 2023) at: https://www.supremecourt.gov/opinions/22pdf/22-506_nmip.pdf and Congressional Research Service at: https://crsreports.congress.gov/product/pdf/IN/IN12350.

302 White House at: https://www.whitehouse.gov/briefing-room/statements-releases/2023/08/22/fact-sheet-the-biden-harris-administration-launches-the-save-plan-the-most-affordable-student-loan-repayment-plan-ever-to-lower-monthly-payments-for-millions-of-borrowers/.

303 Forbes at: https://www.forbes.com/sites/adamminsky/2024/06/20/trump-knocks-bidens-vile-student-loan-forgiveness-plans-suggests-reversal/.

304 Congressional Research Service at: https://crsreports.congress.gov/product/pdf/IN/IN12350.

305 Forbes at: https://www.forbes.com/sites/adamminsky/2024/08/02/notices-on-student-loan-forgiveness--sent-to-40-million-borrowers-with-relief-expected-this-fall/.

306 Forbes at: https://www.forbes.com/sites/adamminsky/2024/06/20/trump-knocks-bidens-vile-student-loan-forgiveness-plans-suggests-reversal/.

307 Department of Education at: https://www.ed.gov/news/press-releases/biden-harris-administration-announces-additional-77-billion-approved-student-debt-relief-160000-borrowers.

308 Forbes at: https://www.forbes.com/sites/adamminsky/2024/06/20/trump-knocks-bidens-vile-student-loan-forgiveness-plans-suggests-reversal/.

309 Congressional Research Service, *Abortion Law Development: A Brief Overview* (2009), accessed at: https://crsreports.congress.gov/product/pdf/RL/95-724.

310 *Roe v. Wade*, 410 U.S. 113 (1973), at: https://tile.loc.gov/storage-services/service/ll/usrep/usrep410/usrep410113/usrep410113.pdf.

311 *Roe v. Wade*, 410 U.S. 113, 154 (1973).

312 *Roe v. Wade*, 410 U.S. 113, 163-64 (1973).

313 *Roe v. Wade*, 410 U.S. 113, 163-64 (1973).

314 *Roe v. Wade*, 410 U.S. 113, 163-65 (1973).

315 *Roe v. Wade*, 410 U.S. 179 (1973), at: https://tile.loc.gov/storage-services/service/ll/usrep/usrep410/usrep410179/usrep410179.pdf.

316 *See* Congressional Research Service, *Abortion Law Development: A Brief*

Overview (2009), accessed at: https://crsreports.congress.gov/product/pdf/RL/95-724.

317 *Planned Parenthood of Southeastern Pennsylvania et. Al. v. Casey,* 505 U.S. 833 (1992), accessed at: https://tile.loc.gov/storage-services/service/ll/usrep/usrep505/usrep505833/usrep505833.pdf.

318 *Planned Parenthood of Southeastern Pennsylvania et. Al. v. Casey,* 505 U.S. 833, 846-53 (1992),

319 *Planned Parenthood of Southeastern Pennsylvania et. Al. v. Casey,* 505 U.S. 833, 864-69 (1992).

320 *Dobbs, State Health Officer of the Mississippi Department of Health et al. v. Jackson Women's Health Organization,* 597 U.S. 215 (2022), accessed at: https://www.supremecourt.gov/opinions/21pdf/19-1392_6j37.pdf.

321 *Brown v. Board of Education of Topeka,* 347 U.S. 483 (1954) accessed at: https://supreme.justia.com/cases/federal/us/347/483/.

322 Supreme Court of the United States, No. 210, October Term, 1895, accessed at: https://www.archives.gov/milestone-documents/plessy-v-ferguson.

323 Gallup, *Where Do Americans Stand on Abortion,* at: https://news.gallup.com/poll/321143/americans-stand-abortion.aspx.

324 Gallup, *Where Do Americans Stand on Abortion,* at: https://news.gallup.com/poll/321143/americans-stand-abortion.aspx.

325 NBC News, *Donald Trump: I was able to kill Roe v. Wade,* at: https://www.nbcnews.com/politics/donald-Donald Trump/Donald Trump-was-able-kill-roe-v-wade-rcna84897.

326 CNN, *Donald Trump says abortion legislation should be left to the states,* at: https://www.cnn.com/2024/04/08/politics/donald-Donald Trump-abortion-2024/index.html.

327 Washington Post, *Donald Trump vows to be "side by side" with group that wants abortion "eradicated"* at: https://www.washingtonpost.com/politics/2024/06/10/Donald Trump-speech-danbury-institute-abortion/.

328 CNN at: https://www.cnn.com/2024/07/17/politics/kfile-J.D.-vance-abortion-comments/index.html.

329 KFF at: https://www.kff.org/global-health-policy/fact-sheet/mexico-city-policy-explainer/.

330 Politico at: https://www.politico.com/news/2024/07/29/kamala-harris-abortion-restoring-roe-00171657.

331 CMS at: https://www.cms.gov/files/document/qso-22-22-hospitals.pdf.

332 KFF at: https://www.kff.org/global-health-policy/fact-sheet/mexico-city-policy-explainer/.

333 Gallup, *Inflation, Immigration Rank Among Top U.S. Issue Concerns,* (March 29, 2024) at: https://news.gallup.com/poll/642887/inflation-immigration-rank-among-top-issue-concerns.aspx.

334 Pew Research Center, *What the data says about crime in the U.S.,* at: https://www.pewresearch.org/short-reads/2024/04/24/what-the-data-says-about-

crime-in-the-us/.

335 Pew Research Center, *What the data says about crime in the U.S.*, at: https://www.pewresearch.org/short-reads/2024/04/24/what-the-data-says-about-crime-in-the-us/; and Congressional Research Service, *Violent Crime Trends, 1990-2021*, IF12281 (Dec. 2022) at https://crsreports.congress.gov/product/pdf/IF/IF12281.

336 Pew Research Center, *What the data says about crime in the U.S.*, at: https://www.pewresearch.org/short-reads/2024/04/24/what-the-data-says-about-crime-in-the-us/; and Congressional Research Service, *Violent Crime Trends, 1990-2021*, IF12281 (Dec. 2022) at https://crsreports.congress.gov/product/pdf/IF/IF12281.

337 Pew Research Center, *What the data says about crime in the U.S.*, at: https://www.pewresearch.org/short-reads/2024/04/24/what-the-data-says-about-crime-in-the-us/; and Congressional Research Service, Violent Crime Trends, 1990-2021, IF12281 (Dec. 2022) at https://crsreports.congress.gov/product/pdf/IF/IF12281.

338 For a graph showing the violent crime and homicide rates over 30 years, see Congressional Research Service, Violent Crime Trends, 1990-2021, IF12281, Figure 1 (Dec. 2022) at: https://crsreports.congress.gov/product/pdf/IF/IF12281

339 Pew Research Center, *What the data says about crime in the U.S.*, at: https://www.pewresearch.org/short-reads/2024/04/24/what-the-data-says-about-crime-in-the-us/.

340 "Mass shootings" refers to 4 or more people killed or injured by a firearm, at: https://everytownresearch.org/mass-shootings-in-america/.

341 Statista, *Number of Mass Shootings in the U.S. between 1982 and 2023*, at: https://www.statista.com/statistics/811487/number-of-mass-shootings-in-the-us/; and *AP*, Donald Trump receives NRA endorsement as he vows to protect gun rights (May 2024), at: https://apnews.com/article/Donald Trump-speech-nra-gun-owners-second-amendment-de03ae7672f2b1e213da6acbf25df378.

342 NPR, *How the U.S. gun violence death rate compares with the rest of the world*, at: https://www.npr.org/sections/goatsandsoda/2023/10/31/1209683893/how-the-u-s-gun-violence-death-rate-compares-with-the-rest-of-the-world.

343 NPR, *How the U.S. gun violence death rate compares with the rest of the world*, at: https://www.npr.org/sections/goatsandsoda/2023/10/31/1209683893/how-the-u-s-gun-violence-death-rate-compares-with-the-rest-of-the-world.

344 Wikipedia, *Estimated number of civilian guns per capita by country based on the Small Arms Survey 2017 in Geneva Switzerland*, at: https://en.wikipedia.org/wiki/Estimated_number_of_civilian_guns_per_capita_by_country#External_links.

345 Northwestern University, *Assault weapon ban significantly reduces mass shooting* (March 2021), at https://news.northwestern.edu/stories/2021/03/assault-weapon-ban-significantly-reduces-mass-shooting/.

346 Statista, *Do you support or oppose banning assault-style weapons* (Jan. 2024) at: https://www.statista.com/statistics/811842/support-distribution-for-banning-assault-style-weapons-in-the-united-states/.

347 Yahoo News, *Donald Trump opposes assault weapons ban*, (Oct 2015) at: https://www.yahoo.com/news/donald-Donald Trump-opposes-assault-weapons-ban-the-bad-140203052.html?fr=sycsrp_catchall.

348 AP, *Donald Trump's strong words on guns give way to political reality* (March 2018), at: https://apnews.com/article/10fec7540e3d44a9aa045b2dad813b97.

349 CNN, *NRA found liable in corruption case as jury says longtime leader Wayne LaPierre should repay $4.3 million* (Feb. 23, 2024), at: https://www.cnn.com/2024/02/23/us/nra-trial-verdict-new-york/index.html.

350 NPR, *Harris calls for renewing the assault weapons ban after Highland Park mass shooting*, at: https://www.npr.org/2022/07/05/1109924708/harris-calls-for-renewing-the-assault-weapons-ban-after-highland-park-mass-shoot.

351 North Atlantic Treaty, accessed at: https://www.nato.int/cps/en/natolive/official_texts_17120.htm.

352 NATO at: https://www.nato.int/cps/en/natohq/declassified_139339.htm.

353 BBC at: https://www.bbc.com/news/world-europe-68397525.

354 Council on Foreign Relations, *Global Conflict Tracker* (updated May 20, 2024), at: https://www.cfr.org/global-conflict-tracker/conflict/conflict-ukraine?ref=atlanticcityfocus.com.

355 NATO, *NATO's response to Russia's invasion of Ukraine* (March 2024) at: https://www.nato.int/cps/en/natohq/topics_192648.htm.

356 Reuters at: https://www.reuters.com/world/europe/putin-rues-soviet-collapse-demise-historical-russia-2021-12-12/.

357 Brookings Institution at: https://www.brookings.edu/articles/the-long-game-chinas-grand-strategy-to-displace-american-order/; and DOD at: https://www.defense.gov/News/News-Stories/Article/Article/3562442/dod-report-details-chinese-efforts-to-build-military-power/.

358 Business Insider, GOP Senate candidate JD Vance said he doesn't 'really care what happens to Ukraine', at: https://www.businessinsider.com/gop-candidate-jd-vance-i-dont-care-what-happens-ukraine-2022-2.

359 Pew Research Center, *Americans' opinions of NATO* (May 2024) at: https://www.pewresearch.org/global/2024/05/08/americans-opinions-of-nato/.

360 White House, *Joint Vision Statement from the Leaders of Japan, the Philippines, and the United States* (April 11, 2024), at: https://www.whitehouse.gov/briefing-room/statements-releases/2024/04/11/joint-vision-statement-from-the-leaders-of-japan-the-philippines-and-the-united-states/.

361 The U.S.-ROK Mutual Defense Treaty was signed in 1953, available

at: https://www.usfk.mil/Portals/105/Documents/SOFA/H_Mutual%20 Defense%20Treaty_1953.pdf. The Treaty of Mutual Cooperation and Security between the U.S. and Japan was signed in 1960, available at: https:// en.wikisource.org/wiki/Treaty_of_Mutual_Cooperation_and_Security_ between_Japan_and_the_United_States_of_America.

362 BBC, *North Korea recently tested intercontinental missile system*, at: https:// www.bbc.com/news/world-asia-60702463.

363 Human Rights Watch, *North Korea, Events of 2023*, at: https://www.hrw.org/ world-report/2024/country-chapters/north-korea.

364 FactCheck.org at: https://www.factcheck.org/2024/02/Donald Trumps-distorted-nato-delinquent-comments/.

365 NBC News, *Donald Trump says he and North Korea's Kim Jong Un "fell in love." Here's how the GOP responded* (Oct. 1, 2018), at: https://www. nbcnews.com/think/opinion/Donald Trump-says-he-north-korea-s-kim-jong-un-fell-ncna915436.

366 CNN, *John Kelly goes on the record to confirm several disturbing stories about Donald Trump*, https://www.cnn.com/2023/10/02/politics/john-kelly-donald-Donald Trump-us-service-members-veterans/index.html.

367 Congressional Research Service, *NATO Enlargement to Sweden and Finland*, IN11949 (March 2024) at: https://crsreports.congress.gov/product/ pdf/IN/IN11949.

368 White House Statement, *Joint Vision Statement from the Leaders of Japan, the Philippines, and the United States* (April 11, 2024) at: https://www. whitehouse.gov/briefing-room/statements-releases/2024/04/11/joint-vision-statement-from-the-leaders-of-japan-the-philippines-and-the-united-states/.

369 White House, *Joint Leaders Statement on AUKUS* (March 13, 2023) at: https://www.whitehouse.gov/briefing-room/statements-releases/2023/03/13/ joint-leaders-statement-on-aukus-2/.

370 White House, *Remarks by President Joe Biden and President Yoon Suk Yeol of the Republic of Korea in Joint Press Conference* (April 26, 2023), at: https://www.whitehouse.gov/briefing-room/speeches-remarks/2023/04/26/ remarks-by-president-Joe Biden-and-president-yoon-suk-yeol-of-the-republic-of-korea-in-joint-press-conference-2/.

371 Statista, There have been more than 1.3 million military fatalities in all major wars involving the United States from 1775 to 2024, at: https://www.statista. com/statistics/1009819/total-us-military-fatalities-in-american-wars-1775-present/.

372 Veteranaid.org at: https://www.veteranaid.org/blog/how-veterans-administration-created-history-of-us-veteran-benefits#.

373 National Park Service at: https://www.nps.gov/articles/000/-with-malice-toward-none-lincoln-s-second-inaugural.htm.

374 The Atlantic at: https://www.theatlantic.com/politics/archive/2020/09/Donald Trump-americans-who-died-at-war-are-losers-and-suckers/615997/.

375 Business Insider at: https://www.businessinsider.com/john-mccain-refused-early-release-as-a-pow-in-vietnam-2018-8.

376 The Atlantic at: https://www.theatlantic.com/politics/archive/2020/09/Donald Trump-americans-who-died-at-war-are-losers-and-suckers/615997/.

377 CNN, *John Kelly goes on the record to confirm several disturbing stories about Donald Trump,* at https://www.cnn.com/2023/10/02/politics/john-kelly-donald-Donald Trump-us-service-members-veterans/index.html.

378 The Atlantic at: https://www.theatlantic.com/magazine/archive/2023/11/general-mark-milley-Donald Trump-coup/675375/.

379 White House at: https://www.whitehouse.gov/briefing-room/statements-releases/2022/08/10/fact-sheet-president-Joe Biden-signs-the-pact-act-and-delivers-on-his-promise-to-americas-veterans/.

380 Yes, cattle are the top source of methane emissions in the U.S., at: https://www.verifythis.com/article/news/verify/environment-verify/cattle-cows-the-top-source-of-methane-emissions-in-united-states/536-8d5bf326-6955-4a9c-8ea5-761d73ba464c.

381 Source: https://news.un.org/en/story/2021/08/1097362.

382 About the IPCC, at: https://www.ipcc.ch/about/.

383 Washington Post, *Five key excerpts from the United Nations' climate change report,* at: https://www.washingtonpost.com/climate-environment/2021/08/10/ipcc-report-un-takeaways/.

384 National Geographic at: https://www.nationalgeographic.com/science/article/arctic-summer-sea-ice-could-be-gone-by-2035.

385 The Guardian, *Too late now to save Arctic summer ice, climate scientists find,* at: https://www.theguardian.com/environment/2023/jun/06/too-late-now-to-save-arctic-summer-ice-climate-scientists-find; and NASA, Warming seas may increase frequency of extreme storms at: https://science.nasa.gov/earth/climate-change/warming-seas-may-increase-frequency-of-extreme-storms/.

386 Unless otherwise noted, the bullet points below are from the following source: National Oceanic and Atmospheric Administration, Climate change impacts are increasing for Americans (November 14, 2023), at: https://www.noaa.gov/news-release/climate-change-impacts-are-increasing-for-americans.

387 Washington Post, The Drowning South-Where Seas Are Rising at Alarming Speed, at: https://www.washingtonpost.com/climate-environment/interactive/2024/southern-us-sea-level-rise-risk-cities/?itid=mr_climate_1.

388 Climate Change: Global Sea Level, at: https://www.climate.gov/news-features/understanding-climate/climate-change-global-sea-level.

389 Michigan Tech at: https://www.mtu.edu/greatlakes/research-highlights/climate-change-great-lakes/.

390 NOAA, *Climate change impacts are increasing for Americans* (November 14, 2023), at: https://www.noaa.gov/news-release/climate-change-impacts-

are-increasing-for-americans.

391 CNN, *Extreme floods are happening way more often than federal data would suggest* (June 27, 2023), at: https://www.cnn.com/2023/06/26/us/extreme-flood-risk-first-street-federal-data-climate/index.html; and PBS New Hour, *Midwestern floods and failing dams,* at: https://www.pbs.org/newshour/show/june-30-2024-pbs-news-weekend-full-episode.

392 NOAA, *Climate change impacts are increasing for Americans* (November 14, 2023), at: https://www.noaa.gov/news-release/climate-change-impacts-are-increasing-for-americans.

393 NOAA, *2023: A historic year for U.S. billion-dollar weather and climate disasters,* at: https://www.climate.gov/news-features/blogs/beyond-data/2023-historic-year-us-billion-dollar-weather-and-climate-disasters.

394 Washington Post, *A year of record global heat has pushed Earth closer to dangerous threshold,* at: https://www.washingtonpost.com/weather/2024/06/05/global-temperatures-1-5-celsius-record-year/.

395 WRI, *10 Big Findings from the 2023 IPCC Report on Climate Change,* at: https://www.wri.org/insights/2023-ipcc-ar6-synthesis-report-climate-change-findings.

396 PBS, *Coal-fired plants will have to capture emissions or shut down, says strict new EPA rule,* at: https://www.pbs.org/newshour/politics/coal-fired-plants-will-have-to-capture-emissions-or-shut-down-says-strict-new-epa-rule.

397 National Geographic, *Renewable energy explained,* at: https://www.nationalgeographic.com/environment/article/renewable-energy.

398 Financial Times, *Bill Gates' TerraPower plans to build first US next-generation nuclear plant,* at: https://www.ft.com/content/418907d1-d497-439c-9800-eb814226ab71.

399 DOE at: https://www.energy.gov/eere/better-buildings/better-buildings.

400 *See* https://www.housebeautiful.com/design-inspiration/home-makeovers/a44845563/should-you-paint-your-roof-white-to-save-energy/.

401 DOE at: https://www.energy.gov/sites/prod/files/2021/03/f83/Advanced%20Transmission%20Technologies%20Report%20-%20final%20as%20of%2012.3%20-%20FOR%20PUBLIC_0.pdf.

402 Nature, *Innovations to decarbonize materials industries,* at: https://www.nature.com/articles/s41578-021-00376-y.

403 Nature, *Ensuring greenhouse gas reductions from electric vehicles compared to hybrid gasoline vehicles requires a cleaner U.S. electricity grid,* at: https://www.nature.com/articles/s41598-024-51697-1.

404 Washington Post, *How water could be the future of fuel,* https://www.washingtonpost.com/climate-solutions/interactive/2024/green-hydrogen-water-clean-fuel-process/.

405 DOT, Public Transportation's Role in Responding to Climate

Change, https://www.transit.dot.gov/sites/fta.dot.gov/files/docs/
PublicTransportationsRoleInRespondingToClimateChange2010.pdf.

406 *What is the relationship between deforestation and climate change*, at: https://
www.rainforest-alliance.org/insights/what-is-the-relationship-between-
deforestation-and-climate-change/.

407 CNN, *A potent planet-warming gas is seeping out of U.S. landfills at rates
higher than previously thought*, at: https://www.cnn.com/2024/03/28/climate/
us-landfills-methane-pollution-climate/index.html.

408 NPR, *Agriculture industry takes steps to reduce methane, a potent
greenhouse gas*, at: https://www.npr.org/2023/07/20/1188869623/agriculture-
industry-takes-steps-to-reduce-methane-a-potent-greenhouse-gas.

409 Newsweek, *What has Donald Trump said about global warming*, at: https://
www.newsweek.com/what-has-Donald Trump-said-about-global-warming-
quotes-climate-change-paris-agreement-618898.

410 BBC, *Climate Change: U.S. formally withdraws from Paris agreement*, at:
https://www.bbc.com/news/science-environment-54797743.

411 Politico at: https://www.politico.com/news/magazine/2021/01/18/Donald
Trump-presidency-administration-biggest-impact-policy-analysis-451479;
and NPR at: https://www.npr.org/2021/04/28/991635101/congress-votes-to-
restore-regulations-on-climate-warming-methane-emissions.

412 Politico at: https://www.politico.com/news/magazine/2021/01/18/Donald
Trump-presidency-administration-biggest-impact-policy-analysis-451479.

413 New York Times, *Senate Democrats Open Inquiry into Donald Trump's $1
Billion Request of Oil Industry*, at: https://www.nytimes.com/2024/05/23/
climate/Donald Trump-oil-democrats.html.

414 Washington Post, *Senate approves Inflation Reduction Act, clinching long-
delayed health and climate bill*, at: https://www.washingtonpost.com/us-
policy/2022/08/07/senate-inflation-reduction-act-climate/.

415 Washington Post, *How the Inflation Reduction Act might affect you – and
change the U.S.*, at: https://www.washingtonpost.com/us-policy/2022/07/28/
manchin-schumer-climate-deal/.

416 Gallup at: https://news.gallup.com/poll/642887/inflation-immigration-rank-
among-top-issue-concerns.aspx.

417 ASCE, *2021 report card marks the nation's infrastructure progress* (March
3, 2021), at: https://www.asce.org/publications-and-news/civil-engineering-
source/civil-engineering-magazine/issues/magazine-issue/article/2021/03/
asce-2021-report-card-marks-the-nations-infrastructure-progress/.

418 Washington Post, *What's in the $1.2 trillion infrastructure law* (Nov. 16,
2021), at: https://www.washingtonpost.com/business/2021/08/10/senate-
infrastructure-bill-what-is-in-it/.

419 Bloomberg, How Donald Trump's $1 Trillion Infrastructure Pledge Added
Up, at: https://www.bloomberg.com/news/articles/2020-11-16/what-did-all-
those-infrastructure-weeks-add-up-to.

420 Bloomberg, How Donald Trump's $1 Trillion Infrastructure Pledge Added Up, at: https://www.bloomberg.com/news/articles/2020-11-16/what-did-all-those-infrastructure-weeks-add-up-to.

421 Washington Post, *What's in the $1.2 trillion infrastructure law* (Nov. 16, 2021), at: https://www.washingtonpost.com/business/2021/08/10/senate-infrastructure-bill-what-is-in-it/.

422 Association of State Dam Safety Officials at: https://damsafety.org/article/legislative/infrastructure-bill-includes-significant%C2%A0funding-dam-safety-programs.

423 Washington Post, A New era of industrial policy kicks off with signing of the Chips Act, at: https://www.washingtonpost.com/us-policy/2022/08/09/micron-40-billion-us-subsidies/.

424 Yahoo Finance, How Donald Trump worsened the semiconductor shortage, at: https://finance.yahoo.com/news/how-Donald Trump-worsened-the-semiconductor-shortage-192026179.html?fr=sycsrp_catchall.

425 Forbes, *U.S. Energy Independence Soars to Highest Level in Over 70 Years* (May 2, 2023), at: https://www.forbes.com/sites/rrapier/2023/05/02/us-energy-independence-soars-to-highest-levels-in-over-70-years/.

426 NYTimes, *Why Gas Prices Are So High* (June 14, 2022), at: https://www.nytimes.com/interactive/2022/06/14/business/gas-prices.html.

427 Former Senator and Vice President Hubert H. Humphrey.

428 For background on Medicaid, *see* https://www.healthinsurance.org/glossary/medicaid/

429 IRS at: https://www.irs.gov/credits-deductions/individuals/earned-income-tax-credit-eitc.

430 Congressional Research Service at: https://crsreports.congress.gov/product/pdf/R/R42505.

431 Congressional Research Service at: https://crsreports.congress.gov/product/pdf/R/R46234.

432 USDA at: https://www.usda.gov/media/press-releases/2023/11/03/wic-vital-vastly-underutilized-research-finds.

433 HUD at: https://www.hud.gov/topics/rental_assistance/phprog.

434 USA.gov at: https://www.usa.gov/housing-voucher-section-8.

435 Social Security Administration at: https://www.ssa.gov/ssi.

436 HHS at: https://www.hhs.gov/answers/programs-for-families-and-children/what-is-tanf/index.html.

437 Congressional Research Service at: https://crsreports.congress.gov/product/pdf/R/R48068 and https://www.vanhollen.senate.gov/news/press-releases/van-hollen-huffman-introduce-bill-to-fully-fund-special-education#.

438 SSA at: https://www.ssa.gov/disability.

439 Benefits.gov at: https://www.benefits.gov/benefit/623.

440 Courts eventually struck down the rule and then it was withdrawn by the Joe Biden Administration. *See* CBS News at: https://www.cbsnews.com/news/

food-stamps-work-requirement-Donald Trump-rule-abandoned/. *See also* Politico at: https://www.politico.com/news/magazine/2021/01/18/Donald Trump-presidency-administration-biggest-impact-policy-analysis-451479.

441 Politico at: https://www.politico.com/news/magazine/2021/01/18/Donald Trump-presidency-administration-biggest-impact-policy-analysis-451479; and CNN at: https://www.cnn.com/2024/04/23/politics/overtime-pay-salaried-workers-Joe Biden/index.html.

442 See Congressional Budget Office estimate at: https://www.cbo.gov/publication/52859.

443 NBC News at: https://www.nbcnews.com/politics/2016-election/donald-Donald Trump-criticized-after-he-appears-mock-reporter-serge-kovaleski-n470016.

444 New York Times at: https://www.nytimes.com/1999/11/28/opinion/liberties-Donald Trump-shrugged.html.

445 White House (March 11, 2024) at: https://www.whitehouse.gov/briefing-room/statements-releases/2024/03/11/the-american-rescue-plan-arp-top-highlights-from-3-years-of-recovery/#.

446 Harris-Walz (Aug. 16, 2024) at: https://mailchi.mp/press.kamalaharris.com/vice-president-harris-lays-out-agenda-to-lower-costs-for-american-families.

447 White House (March 11, 2024), at: https://www.whitehouse.gov/briefing-room/statements-releases/2024/03/11/the-american-rescue-plan-arp-top-highlights-from-3-years-of-recovery/#.

448 Harris-Walz at: https://mailchi.mp/press.kamalaharris.com/vice-president-harris-lays-out-agenda-to-lower-costs-for-american-families.

449 NBC News at: https://www.nbcnews.com/politics/2024-election/trump-harris-taxes-tips-minimum-wage-labor-economy-rcna166224, and https://www.cbo.gov/publication/55681.

450 White House (March 11, 2024), at: https://www.whitehouse.gov/briefing-room/statements-releases/2024/03/11/the-american-rescue-plan-arp-top-highlights-from-3-years-of-recovery/#.

451 Source for the following items is a White House statement on July 26, 2024, *The Biden-Harris Administration Marks the Anniversary of the Americans with Disabilities Act,* at: https://www.whitehouse.gov/briefing-room/statements-releases/2024/07/26/fact-sheet-the-biden-%E2%81%A0harris-administration-marks-the-anniversary-of-the-americans-with-disabilities-act-2/.

452 DOT: https://www.transportation.gov/airconsumer/disabilitybillofrights.

453 Gallup at: https://news.gallup.com/poll/642887/inflation-immigration-rank-among-top-issue-concerns.aspx.

454 H.R. 1 (115th Cong.) at: https://www.congress.gov/bill/115th-congress/house-bill/1/all-actions?overview=closed#tabs.

455 Congressional Budget Office at: https://www.cbo.gov/publication/54994.

456 NBC News at: https://www.nbcnews.com/politics/congress/republicans-kill-border-bill-sign-Donald Trumps-strength-mcconnells-waning-in-rcna137477.

457 White House at: https://www.whitehouse.gov/briefing-room/statements-releases/2022/08/10/fact-sheet-president-Joe Biden-signs-the-pact-act-and-delivers-on-his-promise-to-americas-veterans/.

458 Fiscal Responsibility Act at: https://www.congress.gov/bill/118th-congress/house-bill/3746. *See also Trillions: Federal Spending, Taxes, the U.S. Debt Ceiling, and Fiscal Law* at: www.lexisnexis.com/trillions.

459 New York Times at: https://www.nytimes.com/2024/05/09/us/politics/senate-faa-air-travel.html; and White House at: https://www.whitehouse.gov/briefing-room/statements-releases/2024/05/16/statement-from-president-joe-Joe Biden-after-signing-faa-reauthorization-act/.

460 The Atlantic at: https://www.theatlantic.com/ideas/archive/2024/07/donald-trump-legal-cases-charges/675531/; and CNN at: https://www.cnn.com/2024/05/30/politics/donald-Donald Trump-hush-money-trial-verdict/index.html.

461 The Atlantic at: https://www.theatlantic.com/ideas/archive/2024/07/donald-trump-legal-cases-charges/675531/.

462 On December 4, 2022, Trump called for "the termination of all rules, regulations, and articles, even those found in the Constitution." CNN at: https://www.cnn.com/2022/12/03/politics/trump-constitution-truth-social/index.html.

463 New York Times, *Donald Trump Impeached for Abuse of Power and Obstruction of Congress,* at: https://www.nytimes.com/2019/12/18/us/politics/Donald Trump-impeached.html; and CNN, *House impeaches Trump for "incitement of insurrection"* at: https://www.cnn.com/2021/01/13/politics/house-vote-impeachment/index.html.

464 The Atlantic at: https://www.theatlantic.com/ideas/archive/2024/07/donald-trump-legal-cases-charges/675531/; and CNN, *Trump indicted in Georgia 2020 election subversion probe,* at: https://www.cnn.com/politics/live-news/trump-fulton-county-georgia-08-14-23/index.html.

465 The Atlantic at: https://www.theatlantic.com/ideas/archive/2024/07/donald-trump-legal-cases-charges/675531/; and NYTimes, *Justice Dept. Charges Trump in Documents Case* at: https://www.nytimes.com/2023/06/09/us/politics/trump-indictment-charges-documents-justice-department.html.

466 GAO, U.S. Gov't Accountability Off. Decision, B-331564, (Jan. 16, 2020), at: https://www.gao.gov/assets/710/703909.pdf; and *Trillions: Federal Spending, Taxes, the U.S. Debt Ceiling, and Fiscal Law,* § 5.06, at: www.lexisnexis.com/trillions.

467 **Each of the following quotes are from the report of the** *Select Committee to Investigate the January 6th Attack on the United States Capitol* (December 2022) at: https://docs-cdn-prod.news-engineering.aws.wapo.pub/publish_document/967ead23-9f0d-4fe7-8f27-8d78411e8a2d/published/967ead23-

9f0d-4fe7-8f27-8d78411e8a2d.pdf.

468 PolitiFact.com on court challenges at: https://www.politifact.com/
factchecks/2022/oct/28/instagram-posts/trump-campaigns-evidence-of-
fraud-was-reviewed-bef/; Reuters on recounts at: https://www.reuters.
com/article/fact-check/contrary-to-social-media-posts-recounts-of-the-
2020-us-presidential-election-idUSL2N2WJ1J9/; Senate Roll Call Votes
at: https://www.senate.gov/legislative/LIS/roll_call_votes/vote1171/
vote_117_1_00001.htm and https://www.senate.gov/legislative/LIS/roll_
call_votes/vote1171/vote_117_1_00002.htm; and House Roll Call Votes at:
https://clerk.house.gov/Votes/202110?Page=45 and https://clerk.house.gov/
Votes/202111?Page=45.

469 Bloomberg at: https://www.bloomberg.com/graphics/Donald Trump-
administration-conflicts/.

470 White House at: https://www.whitehouse.gov/briefing-room/presidential-
actions/2021/01/20/executive-order-ethics-commitments-by-executive-
branch-personnel/.

471 *Select Committee to Investigate the January 6th Attack on the United States
Capitol* (December 2022) at: https://docs-cdn-prod.news-engineering.aws.
wapo.pub/publish_document/967ead23-9f0d-4fe7-8f27-8d78411e8a2d/
published/967ead23-9f0d-4fe7-8f27-8d78411e8a2d.pdf.

472 PolitiFact at: https://www.politifact.com/factchecks/2024/jul/18/kamala-
harris/fact-checking-kamala-harris-claim-that-jd-vance-sa/

473 CBS News at: https://www.cbsnews.com/news/unlawful-border-crossings-
drop-5th-straight-month-lowest-level-since-september-2020/.

474 Each congressional committee has two staffs—a majority staff and a smaller
minority staff, depending on which political party holds the majority at the
time.

Made in the USA
Columbia, SC
15 September 2024

41764660R00105